KEN WARREN TEACHES
TEXAS
HOLD'EM

ABOUT THE AUTHOR

Ken Warren has supported himself playing professional poker since he left the Air Force in 1987 and has parlayed that success into a career as a best-selling author of six poker books: *Winner's Guide to Texas Hold'em Poker, Ken Warren Teaches Texas Hold'em, Ken Warren Teaches Texas Hold'em 2, Ken Warren Teaches 7-Card Stud, Winner's Guide to Omaha Poker* and *The Big Book of Poker*.

Warren is the best of the new breed of riverboat poker players, and has the unique distinction of playing in and winning the very first legal poker hand in Mississippi in the 20th century. That landmark hand was kings full of sevens in the big blind position.

————————————

This book is dedicated, with love, to my wife, Olga, who did all of the proofreading and kept me on track to finish it on time. I especially want to thank my close friends and family for their help and editorial advice: Jim Blecher, Wellsville, KS, Sherry Dean, Indianapolis, IN, Tom Rand, Allen, TX, Dan Warren, Olympia, WA, Neil Warren, Las Vegas, NV

KEN WARREN TEACHES
TEXAS HOLD'EM

KEN WARREN

CARDOZA PUBLISHING

Cardoza Publishing is the foremost gaming publisher in the world with a library of more than 200 up-to-date and easy-to-read books and strategies. These authoritative works are written by the top experts in their fields and with more than 10,000,000 books in print, represent the most popular gaming books anywhere.

NEW EDITION

First Printing   November 2009

Copyright © 2003, 2009 by Ken Warren
All Rights Reserved

ISBN 13:978-1-5804-2238-3
ISBN 10:1-5804-2238-1
Library of Congress Control Number: 2009937734

TABLE OF CONTENTS

INTRODUCTION

The purpose of this book is to teach you how to win money at Texas hold'em. The method that I'm going to use is the same method that I would use if I could tutor you in person. I have taught many people how to play the game over the past few years, and I've refined a system that seems to work pretty well. The idea is to learn a few basic principles and techniques in each lesson, then practice them by actually playing in a real game.

After gaining some real-life experience at a hold'em table, you can think about what you've read in the book and how it relates to an actual game. When you feel that you've mastered the lesson, or you fully understand the principle being taught, you can go on to the next lesson. How quickly you work through the book is entirely up to you. You will learn at your own pace, because only you can decide when to move on to the next chapter.

I will start out by teaching you how to deal the game, then how to read the board to determine the best possible hand. Then I'll teach you some basic odds and statistics that apply to the game. This won't be an advanced course in mathematics and permutations. Rather, I'll show you the odds that apply to the game and you're free to take from them what you will. As your understanding of Texas hold'em and skill at playing increases, you will see that there are certain odds and statistics that keep recurring during the play of the game. While it's worth your time to remember some of these, you do not have to memorize entire tables of numbers.

A quick look at the Table of Contents will show you the subjects you'll be learning and the order in which they'll be presented to you. After you learn the basics, I hope you'll take the time to read each chapter separately and then apply what you've learned there in a real game. It's important to stop reading between chapters, play in a few games, and practice your new techniques. When you feel that you've got something down well, you should move on to the next chapter. If you keep applying each chapter's lessons gradually, you will steadily become a better player.

I will start you out playing in a solid, safe, conservative style that will give you a good foundation to build upon. My instructions in the beginning will be purposefully low-risk, giving you the highest probability of success when you do play a hand. This playing style will also keep the fluctuations in your bankroll to a minimum.

INTRODUCTION

Of course, you're free to read the chapters in any order you like, but I believe you will get the most out of this book if you follow the order presented, especially if you're a beginning hold'em player. As an obvious example of why the given order is useful: it's a lot more valuable to you to know how to play on the flop before you learn to play on the river. It's not much help to know how to play on the river without first knowing how to play on the flop.

One of the key distinguishing features of this book is that when I present a lesson, concept, or idea, I provide as many specific examples of hands as it takes to illustrate completely what I mean. There's a rule of thumb in writing that says you should usually not give more than three examples of something.

My years of teaching Texas hold'em have taught me that this game is so complex and its subtleties and nuances are so many that it sometimes takes ten examples to make a point. I hope that after reading a chapter, you never have to ask yourself, "What did he mean by that?"

On a personal note, I want to thank you for purchasing this copy of *Ken Warren Teaches Texas Hold'em*. Many of you are probably familiar with my earlier book, *Winner's Guide to Texas Hold'em*. In the six years between the original publication of the books, a lot has happened to me. I've received many letters, phone calls, e-mails, and comments from my readers and fellow poker players about the book. People have asked me how I'm doing, what I've done since, and what's new in my life. I'll give you some highlights.

First, my hometown newspaper published an article about my book. Soon after, I was on a Saturday afternoon radio show, telling the story of how I came to write the book and answering poker-related questions from call-in listeners. I seemed to become well-known very quickly. When I would go to play poker in my regular cardroom, someone would often take the microphone and yell, "Famous in the house!" Strangers began to introduce themselves to me. I found that when I talked about poker or how I'd play a certain hand, no one interrupted me.

I've traveled around the country a good deal since the publication of my first book, and card players wherever I go seem to recognize me and have kind words to share. In the card room where I now regularly play in Kansas City, players have brought in their copies of the book and asked me for autographs. The treatment I've received from my fans has been very rewarding.

When I wrote my first book, my main goal was to provide easy-to-understand, practical advice that would be of immediate help to the average player. Based on the feedback I've received, I think I achieved that goal. My present goal is to add substantially and qualitatively to the body of poker literature currently available. I want to say something about poker that has not been said before, and I want to say it in a new way. There are many poker books around, and I want my work and my thoughts on the game of Texas hold'em to be the clearest, most informative, and most thorough you can find. I believe this book meets that goal.

To my friends who already have copies of my first book, whether we have yet met or not, I offer my thanks for your support. I have on the drawing board plans for six more poker books after this one, each one very different from the other. I have a lot to say about the great game of Texas hold'em, and I can get only one book out at a time. I am looking forward to a long and mutually beneficial relationship with my readers.

By the time this book comes out, I will have moved to Biloxi, Mississippi, and I invite you to look me up in the Biloxi or Gulfport Grand Casino poker room if you're passing through. You can e-mail me at home any time at kennolga@earthlink.net. I welcome your comments and suggestions for improving this book for future printings.

Ready to win big money at the poker table? Then, without further ado, let's move on and learn the great game of Texas hold'em!

COMMON HOLD'EM HANDS

What are the first three shared cards called in Texas hold'em? What's a straddle? If I say you have a gutshot, do you know what cards you're holding?

If these terms are unfamiliar to you, take a moment to skim through the glossary at the end of this book. We need to be speaking the same language, so we understand what a particular word means when talking about Texas hold'em. This is already known as the jargon, or the "lingo," used among players who know the game well. When we agree on definitions and terms in advance, the communication is faster and easier.

Mnemonics

A **mnemonic** is a trick to help you remember something easily. When you pick two cards at random from a deck of fifty-two cards, there are 1,326 different two-card hands that can be created. Since that's a lot to remember, let's disregard suits (A♥ 9♦ is the same as A♠ 9♣). Now you have just 169 possible hands. It gets easier from there, because many of these hands have nicknames, which are the mnemonics in poker.

If you've played poker before, you know that you have to pay careful attention to what's going on in the game. Anything you can do to make this task easier on yourself helps you concentrate on the more important things, like watching the other players play their hands.

Get into the habit of not looking at your hand until it is your turn to act. When the play passes to you, decide how you want to play the hand. If you muck it, then it's over until the next hand. If you decide to play, memorize the hand, place it in front of you with a chip on it to protect it, and then don't look at it again until the hand is over.

Why shouldn't you look at your hand again? Tells will be covered in a later chapter, but you should know now that there are a few tells associated with how you look at your hand and how your opponents react to the flop.

When the flop is all of one suit, you will often see another player immediately double-check his hole cards. This reaction usually means that he has exactly one card of that suit and he's checking to see which one of his hole cards it is. So you know that he does not yet have the flush. Don't do your opponents any favors by providing them with similar knowledge about your hand.

COMMON HOLD'EM HANDS

Let's get back to those mnemonics. Some hands have popular, easy-to-remember names, which help you memorize the hand. The following is a list of all the ones that I know ("s" represents suited cards):

HOLD'EM HAND NICKNAMES	
A A	American Airlines, Pocket Rockets, Eyes of Texas
A K	Big Slick, Santa Barbara
A J	Ajax, Foamy Cleanser
A 10	Johnny Moss
A 8	Dead Man's Hand
A 3 (3 A)	Baskin Robbins
K♥Q♥	Marriage
K J	Kojack
K 10	Katie, Katy
K 9	Canine, Pedigree, Mongrel
K 8	Kokomo
K 7	Columbia River
K 3	King Crab, Alaska Hand
Q Q	Siegfried and Roy
Q J	Maverick
Q 10	Quint, Goolsby
Q 9	Quinine
Q 7	Computer Hand

Q 3	San Francisco Busboy (Queen with a Trey)
J 5	Motown (Jackson 5)
10 5 (5 10)	Woolworth, Barbara Hutton, Dimestore
10 4	Broderick Crawford
10 3	Weinberg
10 2	Doyle Brunson
9 8	Oldsmobile
9 6	Joe Bernstein
9 5	Dolly Parton
9 3 (3 9)	Jack Benny
9 2	Montana Banana
8 8	Little Oldsmobile, Mighty Wurlitzer, Snowmen
8 5	Finky Dink
8 3 (3 8)	Raquel Welch
7 6	Union Oil, Trombones
7 5 (5 7)	Heinz (57 Sauce), Pickle Man
7 2	Beer Hand
6 5s	Ken Warren
6 3	Blocky
6 2	Ainsworth
5 4	Jesse James, Jane Russell
5 3	Bully Johnson
4♠ 4♣	Darth Vader (Dark Fours, Dark Force), Sailboats
4 2 (2 4)	Lumberman's Hand (2 by 4)
3 3	Crabs

HOW TO PLAY TEXAS HOLD'EM

Betting Limits

Texas hold'em is played for a wide variety of limits. What all of these limits have in common is that they adhere to the same betting structure, which is a 1:2 betting ratio. The bets before the flop and on the flop will be exactly one small bet (the lower betting tier), and the bets on the turn and river will be exactly one big bet (the higher betting tier–twice the small bet).

The most common limits for the small and big bets are $1/$2, $2/$4, $3/$6, $4/$8, $5/$10, $10/$20, $15/$30, $20/$40, $30/$60, $60/$120, $100/$200, and $300/$600. You must bet exactly the predetermined amount, which is why it's known as a structured game. You are not free to bet, for example, $4 or $5 in a $3/$6 game. I've been asked why there are no $25/$50 and $50/$100 limit hold'em games. I've looked into it and no one seems to know. It seems to be just a matter of convention.

Another betting structure that's common at lower limits is called spread limit. A spread limit betting structure gives you more freedom—it allows you to bet any amount you choose at any time, as long as that amount is within the preset minimum and maximum.

The most common spread limit is $1/$5, meaning that you can bet any amount from $1 to $5. As in all other poker games, a raise must be at least the amount of the previous bet. There are a few significant differences between playing strategy and tactics in a spread limit game and in a structured game. We'll cover those in a later chapter.

Another popular betting structure is called $1/$4/$8/$8 limit. It's really a form of spread limit with some structure: you can bet from $1 to $4 before and after the flop and from $1 to $8 on the turn and the river.

Number of Players

Texas hold'em can be played with as few as two and as many as twenty-two players. People generally look for tables with ten players, and many Las Vegas poker rooms even play eleven-handed. I believe that the best number of players to have at the table is seven or eight; I'll explain why in a later chapter.

High Hand Wins

Hold'em is played high only. The standard high hand always wins. There are no wild cards. Remember, the final poker hand is made up of exactly five cards.

Small Blind and Big Blind

Blinds are players who are forced to put money in the pot before the cards are dealt. The casino uses blinds to force action from the first two players to the left of the dealer. The **big blind** is always the same amount as the small bet and the **small blind** is one-half of the big blind. For example, the blinds in a $4/$8 game would be $2 in the small blind and $4 in the big blind. An exception is a $1/$4/$8/$8 limit game, in which the big blind is $2 and the small blind is $1.

In a game where the small blind can't be exactly half of the big blind, it's usually rounded down. For example, the blinds in a $3/$6 game should be $3 and $1.50 but, since a half-dollar is not a betting denomination, the blinds are $3 and $1. The same principle applies in a $15/$30 game where the blinds should be $15 and $7.50. The small blind is rounded down, so the blinds are $15 and $5, or three red chips and one red chip. Did you notice that a $3/$6 game is the same as a $15/$30 game, with only the color of the chips being different?

The purpose of having two blinds is to create a situation where two of the players will have random hands, since they put their money in the pot before seeing their hands, and other players will have voluntarily entered the pot after looking at their hands. This mix of totally random hands and the hands that the other players wish to play against them is designed to create a contest for the pot when the flop comes. Because of the two blind feature of the game, there is no ante in Texas hold'em as there is in stud or draw poker.

Play of the Game

Each player is dealt two cards face down. These cards are called the pocket cards. Do not show these cards to any other player, since they constitute your entire private hand.

Remember that the blinds have to put their bets in the pot before the deal. The play now starts with the player to the immediate left of the big blind and moves clockwise. Each player has three options. He can **fold** (**muck** his hand), **call** (keep his hand and put the correct amount of money in the pot), or **raise** (increase the bet by at least as much as the previous bet).

If no one has raised by the time the action comes back to the small blind, he can either fold, call (put in enough money to make up the difference between his bet and the big blind's bet), or raise at least the amount of the big blind. For example, in a $1/$4/$8/$8 game where the big blind is $2, a raise of $1 is not permitted, because all raises in poker must be for at least the amount of the previous bet.

In a structured game, the raise must be exactly the small-tiered amount. Since the blinds had to put their money in the pot before they saw their hands, they also have the option of raising themselves.

If no one has raised by the time the action gets back around to the big blind, he then has the option to raise. The dealer will ask him, "Option?" and the big blind has to answer with either "**Check**" ("I bet nothing more") or "I raise."

The Flop

After this first betting round is completed, the dealer burns the top card (removes it from play), and turns the next three cards face up on the board. This is the **flop**. There is a second round of betting, beginning with the small blind or the first player in the hand after the small blind if he's out. This round is played with a small bet and three raise limit. Players may check (bet nothing) and pass on to the next player until someone bets.

Once a bet is made, however, players must either call the bet, raise, or fold and go out of play for the remainder of the hand. Checking is no longer an option once a bet is made. This rule holds true for all future rounds of play. Some poker rooms have a four raise or even a five raise limit, so it's wise to know the limits before you start playing.

The Turn

After the second betting round, the dealer burns another card, and then turns the next card face up on the table. This fourth community card is called the **turn**. A third round of betting among the remaining players follows, only this time you can bet from $1 to

$8 in the $1/$4/$8/$8 game or the higher amount in the structured game. For example, in a $3/$6 game you must now bet or raise in $6 increments.

The River

After the action is completed on the turn, the dealer again burns the top card. He now turns a fifth, and final, card face up on the board. There is a final round of betting, called the **river**, which follows the same betting guidelines as the turn.

The Showdown

When all the action is completed, there is a showdown. All the active players who want to claim the pot turn their hands face up. Using his pocket cards and the five cards on the board, each player (with the dealer) determines his best poker hand. The highest hand at the table wins.

The dealer button then moves one player to the left, marking the new dealer's position. The blinds are posted by the next two players, and the game begins all over again.

4

READING THE BOARD

One of the best features of Texas hold'em is that you always know what the best possible hand is at any stage of the game. Before the flop, when all you have are your two hole cards, a pair of aces is the best possible hand. If the hand were over at that point, you'd always win. There's no way to beat pocket aces with only two cards. If you had pocket kings, you would still win most of the time, because the odds against someone's holding pocket aces when you hold kings (against nine opponents) are 19.5-1.

Reading the Flop

The cards that come on the flop tell you which way the hand is headed. With only three cards out there, you can tell immediately what is the best possible hand. If you play in a live game where you're seeing thirty to thirty-five flops an hour, you'll have plenty of opportunity to learn to read the board. It will soon become second nature to you.

Let's look at some sample flops and practice determining the best possible hand.

1. K♥ K♣ J♣

Any time the flop contains a pair, the best possible hand will be either four of a kind or a full house, depending on whether you can account for one of the key cards. If you have no other information, the best possible hand for this flop is four kings. If you have one of the kings in your hand, you know no one else can make four of a kind, and therefore the best possible hand can be only a full house. Anyone holding a king and a jack would have the nuts at that point.

2. 7♠ 7♥ 5♣

The best possible hand is four 7s (7♣, 7♦), followed by 7s full of 5s (7, 5) and then 5s full of 7s (5, 5).

3. 8♠ 8♣ 8♥

It's obvious that the best possible hand with this flop is four 8s. Anyone holding the 8♦ has four 8s regardless of what his other card is. The real question here is what are the second and third best possible hands if you don't have four 8s? Pocket aces and then pocket kings, of course. They each make a full house.

4. K♥ 7♥ 2♥

Any time there are three cards of the same suit on the flop, the best possible hand will be a flush. If those three cards are within five ranks of each other, the best possible hand will be a straight flush. Anyone holding the A♥ and any other heart has the nuts with this flop. If no one has two hearts in his hand, the next best hand would be a possible straight, and then three of a kind.

5.   Q♠ 9♠ 7♠
The best possible hand is the A♠ and any other spade.

6.   6♣ 4♣ 2♣
If you said that the best possible hand is the A♣ and any other club, you'd be wrong. Any player holding 3♣ 5♣ has a straight flush.

7.   5♠ 6♣ 9♥
Whenever the three cards on the flop are within five ranks of each other, a straight is possible. In this example, anyone holding a 7 and an 8 has a straight.

8.   A♦ 5♠ 3♣
Again, a straight is the best possible hand here. Anyone holding a 2 and a 4 has the straight and cannot be beaten at this point.

9.   K♥ J♦ 10♠
The best hole cards you can have with this flop are an ace and a queen, to make a straight. Notice that you can also make a straight with a queen and a 9, but those cards don't make the nut straight.

10.   A♣ 9♥ 6♦
No straight is possible here. The best possible hand is three aces, followed by three 9s and then three 6s.

11.   J♥ 9♣ 5♠

Again, no straight is possible. The best possible hand is three jacks, followed by three 9s, and then three 5s.

12.   7♣ 4♥ 2♦

Pocket 7s are the best cards to be holding, to make three 7s. Next best are pocket 4s, and then pocket 2s.

Reading the Turn

Reading the hands becomes a bit more difficult once an extra card hits the table. Let's make sure you get plenty of practice. Starting with the next hand and continuing through the rest of this chapter, you should try to figure out what the first through the fourth best hands are. I want you to go down to the fourth best hand because although the best and second-best hands will often be obvious, it takes a little more analysis to figure out the next few hands after that.

13.   5♠ 6♣ 9♥ 6♦

The best four hands here are four 6s, 9s full of 6s, 6s full of 9s, and 6s full of 5s.

14.   A♦ 5♦ 3♣ 3♥

The best hands are four 3s, aces full of 3s, 5s full of 3s, and 3s full of aces.

15.   K♥ J♦ 10♠ Q♠

The best hands are an ace-high straight (an ace and any other card), a king-high straight (a 9 and any lower card), three kings, and three queens.

16.   A♣   9♥   6♦   8♣

The best hands are 7 10 to make a 10-high straight, 7 5 to make a 9-high straight, three aces, and three 9s.

17.   J♥   9♣   5♠   K♥

The best hands with this board are a queen and a 10 to make a king-high straight, three kings, three jacks, and three 9s.

18.   7♣   4♥   2♦   5♥

A 6 and an 8 make an 8-high straight, a 6 and a 3 make a 7-high straight, an ace and a 3 make a **wheel**, and pocket 7s make three 7s.

19.   K♥   7♥   2♥   2♦

The best possible hands are four deuces, kings full of deuces, 7s full of deuces, then deuces full of kings.

20.   Q♠   9♠   7♠   9♣

The best hand is four 9s, followed by queens full of 9s, 9s full of queens, and 9s full of 7s. 7s full of 9s, which is ordinarily a powerful hand, is only the fifth best hand with this board.

21.   6♣   4♣   2♣   8♣

Any time the board contains cards of all the same suit, you should look first for the possibility of a straight flush. The best possible hole cards here are the 7♣ and the 5♣ to make an 8-high straight flush. The next best hand is 5♣ 3♣ to make a 6-high straight flush, and best hand after that is the A♣ and any other card.

If you said that three 8s is the fourth best hand, you'd be wrong. It's the K♣ and any other card. If no clubs are out among the players' hands (which often happens with a board like this), the next best hand is an 8-high straight with a 5 and a 7 of other suits.

22.   K♥ K♣ J♣ J♥
The best possible hand is four kings, then four jacks. Third is kings full of jacks, and then jacks full of kings.

Test Your Knowledge #1
What's the fifth best possible hand in #22?
Answer at the end of the chapter.

---

23.   7♠ 7♥ 5♣ 10♠
The best possible hand here is four 7s, followed by 10s full of 7s, 7s full of 10s, and 7s full of 5s. Notice that an ordinarily powerful hand like 5s full is very vulnerable given this flop, where all of the other cards on the board are higher than the 5. Low pocket pairs flop low sets, which in turn make low full houses. We saw a similar situation above, in Example #20.

24.   8♠ 8♣ 8♥ J♣
Sometimes the best possible hand isn't that hard to figure out. The J♣ didn't add anything that could beat four 8s, so four 8s is still the nuts. After that it's jacks full, 8s full of aces, and then 8s full of kings.

Reading the River

We've made it to the last betting round now. If you've practiced enough, you should still be able to predict the four best hands in each example below, even with five cards on the table.

25.   5♠ 6♣ 9♥ 6♦ Q♣

The best possible hand here is four 6s, followed by queens full, 9s full, and then 6s full of queens.

26.   A♦ 5♦ 3♣ 3♥ 4♦

The nuts here is a 5-high straight flush, then four 3s, aces full of 3s, and then 5s full of 3s.

27.   K♥ J♦ 10♠ Q♠ A♠

Anyone holding the K♠ and the J♠ has a royal flush. The second best hand is the K♠ and any other spade. The third best is the J♠ and any other lower spade. The fourth best hand is the 9♠ and any other lower spade.

> *Test Your Knowledge #2*
> If no one at the table is holding two spades, what is the best hand anyone could have?
> Answer at the end of the chapter.

28.   A♣ 9♥ 6♦ 8♣ 3♣

The best possible hand here is the K♣ and any other club, followed by the Q♣ and any lower club, then the J♣ and any lower club, and finally, the 10♣ and any lower club. If no one holds two clubs, then the best possible hand is a 10 and a 7, to make a straight.

29.   J♥ 9♣ 5♠ K♥ 9♥

The best possible hand is a king-high straight flush, if you hold the Q♥ and 10♥. The second-best hand is four 9s, followed by kings full of 9s, and then jacks full of 9s.

30.   7♣ 4♥ 2♦ 5♥ 7♥

A 6♥ and an 8♥ make a straight flush. After that, the best possible hands are four 7s, 7s full of 5s, and then 7s full of 4s.

31.   K♥ 7♥ 2♥ 2♦ 7♦

The best possible hand is four 7s, followed by four deuces. The third best is kings full of 7s, then 7s full of kings.

32.   Q♠ 9♠ 7♠ 9♣ 7♣

The best possible hand here is four 9s, then four 7s, followed by queens full of 9s, and 9s full of queens.

33.   6♣ 4♣ 2♣ 8♣ 4♦

If your hole cards are the 7♣ and the 5♣, you have the nut straight flush. The 5♣ 3♣ is the next best hand to make another straight flush. The third best possible hand is four 4s followed by 8s full of 4s.

34. K♥ K♣ J♣ J♥ 8♥

The best possible hand is four kings, followed by four jacks. Kings full of jacks is the third best, followed by jacks full of kings. Because of the two overpair on the board, the flush card on the river makes the ace-high flush only the sixth best possible hand.

> *Test Your Knowledge #3*
> What is the fifth best possible hand?
> Answer at the end of the chapter.

35. 7♠ 7♥ 5♣ 10♠ J♠

You'd have the nuts if you held the 8♠ and 9♠, to make the jack-high straight flush. The next best possible hand is four 7s, followed by jacks full of 7s, and then 10s full of 7s.

36. 8♠ 8♣ 8♥ J♣ A♥

Since there's no possible way to make a straight flush out of this, the best possible hand is still four 8s. The next best hand is aces full of 8s, followed by jacks full of 8s and then—can you guess? 8s full of aces.

Zero Boards

Often there will be no straight, flush, or full house possible after the river card hits the board. No three cards will be within five ranks of each other, there won't be three or more cards of the same suit, and the board will not be paired. These boards are called **zero boards**. The highest possible hand will always be exactly three of a kind. Zero boards not only are easy to read, they also help you quickly figure out what your opponents might be holding.

Here are a few examples of zero boards:

37. A♠ K♦ 9♦ 6♣ 4♠
The best possible hands here are three aces, three kings, three 9s, and then three 6s. The same logic applies in the next three examples.

38. K♣ J♠ 8♥ 5♥ 3♣

39. A♥ 2♦ 6♥ 7♠ J♣

40. A♣ K♥ 9♦ 8♠ 4♣

Since you don't have to worry about the possibility of a straight, a flush, or a full house, all you have to do is think about the likelihood that your opponent has flopped a set against you. If there was a lot of raising before the flop and the preflop raiser continues betting throughout the hand, then you can usually safely assume that he has a set of aces or kings, given a zero board such as Examples #37 or #40.

If you hold 3♥ 3♦ with a board like Example #38, and there wasn't any preflop raising, nor much action in the hand, then you can assume that your set of 3s is the best hand.

In case you haven't noticed by now, Examples #13 through #24 are the same as Examples #1 through #12, only I have added the turn card. Examples #25 through #36 are the same as the turn card examples, only I have added the river card.

Answers to Test Your Knowledge Questions #1-3

1. You've done everything you can with the kings and the jacks. You have to create some new cards. The answer is pocket aces to make two pair: aces over kings.

2. The answer is any two cards you use to call the final bet and turn face up on the table. You are all playing the straight on the board.

3. After you account for all of the possible four of a kinds, you then look for all possible full houses before you start looking for flushes. Although kings full of 8s and jacks full of 8s are both possible, a player who had either of those hands would also have, respectively, kings full of jacks and jacks full of kings, so those hands would not count. 8s full of kings is the fifth best hand. Notice that the same logic applies to 8s full of jacks (the player would also have jacks full of kings), which is why the ace-high flush is the sixth best hand.

KEEPING RECORDS

Poker is an easy game to learn, but it's a difficult game to master. It is estimated that of all the people who play poker seriously, only one out of twenty is a regular winner in the long run. Nineteen out of twenty players are life-long losers at the poker table. It's not that these nineteen players are idiots, or can't learn the game, or can't read poker books to try to learn to play better. Most poker players have great intelligence, and a lot of them do read poker books and magazines to improve their games. The problem is the game of poker itself. Poker, while being deceptively easy to deal, is extremely hard to play correctly all the time.

There are easily over one hundred separate skills you must master to become an expert poker player. Every skill that you master will have a positive impact on your game in two ways. First, when you possess a particular skill that you can use against your opponents, and your opponents do not have that same skill, you will win money from them (in the long run) in those situations. Second, when you possess that skill and your opponent does also, you will not lose any money to him (again, in the long run) when that particular situation arises.

In other words, having certain skills will make you money when the other players don't have those skills and it will keep you from losing money when they do have those skills. When you hear people say that a certain player has a "leak" in his game, they mean that he lacks a certain important skill, which is why he's losing a lot of money.

What does this discussion have to do with keeping records? I have taught many people how to play Texas hold'em. I also know many self-taught poker players. Between the two groups, I know a lot of poker players, and I think I know who the overall winners and losers are. I'm sure that most of these players are keenly interested in improving their games, and I know they work hard at it.

In all my years of teaching the game, I've seen everything that a player will do to improve his game. The thing that stands out most is that the players who go on to become winners in the long run—that one player out of twenty—are the ones who kept records of their poker playing from the very beginning.

Learning any game and then practicing it until you become a master is very hard. It doesn't matter if it's chess, tennis, bridge, or poker. The process requires self-analysis, self-criticism, introspection, attention to detail, concentration, and, probably most importantly, the ability to be brutally honest with yourself and tolerate hearing unpleasant facts about yourself.

If you keep records of your poker sessions, you'll see that those brutally honest unpleasant facts about yourself that I'm talking about will come from the times that you lost at poker and then actually recorded your loss in your ledger. Players who are willing to do this are the ones who have what it takes to go on to be winners at hold'em.

Now that you've decided you're going to be a hold'em winner, what kind of records should you keep? You're limited only by your imagination and the time that you're willing to put into record-keeping. You can make them as detailed or as basic as you like. Here's a list of suggested categories to put in your poker records:

1. *Where did you play?* If you're lucky enough to have a choice of casino poker rooms near you, note the name and the street address of the one you visited.

2. *What game did you play?* This could be Texas hold'em, 7-Card Stud, Omaha, or any other poker game.

3. *What limit did you play?* Although many limits exist, you most likely will be entering something like $3/$6 or $1/$4/$8/$8, since you'll be playing at the beginning lower limits.

4. *How long did you play?* This statistic is the actual time you spent at the table, in the game. Do not count that hour you went to lunch or all of your excessive short absences from the table. Make this entry in terms of quarter hours. If you can, narrow it down to tenths of an hour. The more accurate your records are, the more valid your results will be when you analyze them.

5. *Calendar date.* This one's always a number between 1 and 31 (some date from the first of the month to the thirty-first of the month). This will also be useful for later analysis.

6. *Day of the week.* M, T, W, R, F, S, U. R is for Thursday and U is for Sunday. As you'll see in the next chapter, this is a very important note to keep.

7. *Time of day.* Record the time that you started playing and the time that you quit playing. Keep this number separate from the total number of hours played in #4, above. They are very different statistics.

8. *How much did you win or lose?* Although this may be the bottom line number that you focus on after each playing session, it is by no means the only statistic of use to you.

9. *Your win/loss converted into # of big bets.* Experienced poker players talk about their wins and losses in terms of how many big bets they won or lost, because that's really the best way to communicate all of the

relevant information. If someone tells you, "I won $200 playing poker the other night," he hasn't really told you as much as he could. You don't know if he was playing $1/$5 for two hours and was extremely lucky, or if he was playing $5/$10 for eight hours and won that $200 on just the last hand he played before leaving the game. Speaking in terms of big bets also makes it easier to compare how you're doing in different games at varying limits.

10. *Hourly rate for this game.* Divide your win or loss for this session by the number of hours you played. If you played eight hours and won $120, then your hourly rate would be a plus $15 per hour. If you were playing $3/$6 limit, this rate would convert to 2.5 big bets per hour.

11. *Hourly rate for all games and totals.* This calculation is the total of all the poker games you've played (regardless of the type of game or the limit) divided by the total number of hours you've played poker. You'll be mixing together all of your stud games with your hold'em games, but, for the purposes of this statistic, it doesn't matter.

The items listed above should be the bare minimum of your records. How much more information you want to collect is practically unlimited and, of course, up to you. Theoretically, the more information you have with which to make decisions, the better your decisions should be. A few more items that might help you are:

12. *Who else is at the table?* If you have a few known **rocks**, or a few habitually bad players in the game, then you know that your results may not truly be representative of an average session for you. Making a note of that will make you feel better, especially if you had a loss that session.

13. *Type of table.* Was it a very loose table, or was it full of no-action rocks? You might want to create a rating system that you understand to help you quantify this quality. You could rate the table on a scale from 1 to 10 with 1 being the tightest table in the world, 5 being average, and 10 being the loosest game you've ever seen. Use whatever works for you.

14. *How well did you play?* Understand that this is not related to how much you actually won or lost. It has to do only with how well you played the game. Did you do your best? Did you go on tilt? How disciplined were you?

15. *Secondary expenses.* If you're going to have a hobby, you might as well know how much it's really costing you. Does it cost you anything to get to the game? Bus fare? Road tolls? If you play in the Chicago area, highway or bridge tolls might be a regular expense. Valet parking? Do you want to count these costs as poker related expenses? Maybe you'd like to keep track of them anyway, without counting them as expenses or losses.

16. *Dealer tokes.* You'd be amazed at how much this can add up to if you give it a little thought. If you play forty hours a week, dealer tips could be as much as $8,000 per year, depending on your style of play and what kind of tipper you are. Whatever they add up to, I strongly recommend that you keep track of them. Apart from being a losing player, they're the single biggest drain on your overall bottom line.

17. *Cocktail waitress tips.* This can also be a big expense for some people. These tips come out of the stack of poker chips that you have in front of you, so write them down.

18. *Narrative remarks.* This section is for anything you want to say about the game that can't be reduced to numbers, or for remarks expanding upon and explaining any of the above entries. I use it as a diary-like entry so that I can give each poker playing session it's own unique characteristics. After reading everything I have on a session, I'm able to remember playing that session, even if it was several years ago.

19. *Tournament results.* Poker tournaments are very different from regular ring games. These records should be kept separate from non-tournament notes. Be sure to record all the same information as in your regular games, but keep it in a separate ledger or file.

How often you take notes is up to you. I would say that the best guideline is: write it down before you forget it. Some people take notes and update them every time they get the dealer button. That's about once every twenty minutes. Some players take notes while the dealer is being replaced by a new dealer. That's exactly once every thirty minutes. Most players wait until after their playing session is over and then take their notes when they get home, either the same day or the next day. Do whatever works for you.

I recommend that you carry a pen and a small writing tablet with you at all times. There are poker rooms that don't allow electronic devices to be used at the table. This includes pocket calculators, voice recorders and palm-sized electronic notepads.

Personally, I carry a small, state-of-the-art digital voice recorder that I step away from the table to use when the dealers are changing. I know another player who sets up a laptop computer on an unused hold'em table nearby, so he can update his notes every hour or so. Incidentally, this player is far superior to me in skill, so, while you're taking a note from me, maybe I should take a note from him. Couldn't hurt.

Future Records

If you're going to be a serious, winning hold'em player, you'll be taking a lot of notes. This book is intended for beginning and novice hold'em players, and I realize that you might feel like you're being burdened for reasons that you really don't understand or care about. I want to assure you that as your skill at hold'em increases (along with your desire to excel), you will be glad that you kept detailed records.

When you pass the beginner stage and approach the point where you are a solid, advanced level player, you'll see that the statistics you've kept will be even more useful to you than you could imagine right now. You will be able to calculate things like standard deviation, confidence intervals, bankroll requirements, chance of going broke, expectation, standard error, variance, and several other things that probably don't mean anything to you right now.

My recommendation is: keep the detailed records now, even if you don't understand them all, because one day you will understand them, and you'll be glad you kept the detailed records.

Final Advice

Don't forget that you're just a beginner. Don't be too hard on yourself. When you start playing hold'em seriously and you're keeping records, you might get discouraged when you have to record loss after loss. This might keep you from wanting to play the game at all. I want you to allow yourself a training period where we will agree in advance that your results don't matter. After all, it's a training period. Nobody can expect to be a big winner while he's still learning, no matter what the subject is.

Give yourself a break. Decide how long you want to take as your learning period. During that time, concentrate on improving as a player and don't worry too much about the results. Of course, you'd like to see an upward trend after a while, but you should be more concerned about increasing your understanding of the game. When you feel like you're no longer a beginner, start your records over with a zero balance, as if you had never played before. Don't forget to have fun!

Structure Your Learning

Assignment #1

Here we are at the end of the fifth chapter of a book entitled *Ken Warren Teaches Texas Hold'em*, and you're probably thinking, "How is anybody going to teach me anything if I don't have any homework assignments?" Your wishes will be granted, starting right now. All of the material presented up to this point was necessary to teach you the basics about poker and Texas hold'em. Now that you have some of the basics under your belt, we can change our focus from the broad and general to the more narrow and specific aspects of the game.

Your first assignment is to create a file, folder, ledger, logbook, or notebook for keeping your poker records. It can be anything from a memo pad with just the basics to a computer file with every category you can imagine. It has to meet just three main criteria: it must contain your own personal records, they must be permanent, and you must be able to update them easily whenever you wish to.

If you have no idea how you want to create this record, then I suggest you use an 8.5" x 11" notepad. Following the eighteen categories listed above, number your lines 1 through 18 and fill in the blanks. Use the rest of the page for narrative remarks. Your notepad will have 50, 75 or 100 sheets, and you will be using one sheet per playing session. By the time you run out of sheets, you will know what is most comfortable for you. You'll either start with another tablet or you might switch to a computer-generated spreadsheet or program. Good luck.

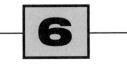

PLAYING CALENDAR

If you're a typical hold'em player, you probably have a job, a family, and a home to take care of. You're not free to go play poker for hours on end any time the mood strikes you. You have to budget your time. You have to plan ahead so that you can get the most value and pleasure from your poker playing time. That's how this chapter will help you.

If you play in a regularly scheduled poker game at a friend's home, there's not much you can do about changing the day or the time the game starts. If you're not there for the game, you don't get to play. If you play in a casino poker room, however, or if you're lucky enough to have a choice of more than one poker room to visit, then you have some decisions to make.

Every hour you spend in a hold'em game is not necessarily equal to every other hour you play. In poker, as in most aspects of life, one day of the week is not the same as every other day of the week. A poker game changes over time. It is like a living, breathing organism that evolves into something else every time a player leaves the game or a new player is seated. You can predict in advance which times are better than others if you know which factors to consider. Let's look at a list of those now:

1. *What day of the week is it?* Most people have already realized the importance of this question. Everybody knows that Saturday is always better than Tuesday, just because the majority of people who have jobs usually work Monday through Friday.

2. *Is Monday a holiday?* When Monday is a holiday, the games are just as good on Monday as they are on Saturday and Sunday.

3. *Is it Monday evening?* If it's Monday night during football season, the poker room usually has giveaways and specials for the poker players. You might get to enter a free football pool or have a shot at extra money added to the jackpot.

4. *What day of the month is it?* The 15th and the 30th or 31st are Federal Government paydays, and Social Security recipients get their checks on the last day of the month. If that's a Monday, then the previous Friday, Saturday, and Sunday are what's known as "hot-check days," because everyone can write a check and know it will be good by the time it makes it to the bank on Monday or later.

5. *Is it Friday?* Besides being the last day of the traditional workweek, Fridays are good for poker players because a lot of people get their paychecks on Friday.

6. *What time of day is it?* Games played during the mornings and afternoons tend to be full of older, more conservative players, who have a lot of playing experience. The pots at those times will be smaller than average, and you won't get paid off as well on your winning hands. Evening and late night players tend to be younger and a little looser, so there's a lot more action in those games. Your opponents at those times will be making more mistakes when they play against you.

7. *How big is the jackpot? Is it double or triple jackpot night?* If the jackpot is unusually large, then it might be worth your time to play, even if it's a time when you wouldn't ordinarily go. Some cardrooms double or even triple the jackpot (up to a certain amount) on Tuesdays, Wednesdays, or Thursdays in an effort to increase business.

8. *Is it tournament night?* Originally, one of the main purposes of tournaments was to draw players to the cardroom, so they would fill the ring games as they were eliminated from the tournament. It still works. That's why there are more tournaments on a poker room's slow days than there are on the busy days.

9. *Personal obligations.* There's an old joke with the punch line: "On Mondays, Wednesdays and Fridays, when I attend my Alcoholics Anonymous meetings, we play poker. On Tuesdays and Thursdays, when I attend my Gamblers Anonymous meetings, we sit around and drink." Whatever your personal obligations are during the week, don't forget them. Take them into consideration when deciding when to play.

Structure Your Learning

Assignment #2

If you read this chapter, and you recall that its title is "Playing Calendar," then you probably know what's coming. I want you to create your own personalized playing calendar. Using a monthly calendar (either a commercially published calendar or one that is generated by computer), figure out which days of the month would be best for you to play hold'em. Use the criteria listed above and anything else you want to add to assign each day a relative value.

Perhaps you could give each day one point for each of the factors that mean the most to you, and then arrange the days from best to worst. Then you could grade each day using an "A," "B," or "C" for easy reference. Use the system that works best for you. The purpose of this exercise is to get you to think ahead, so you can make the best of your poker playing time. You should also write the phone numbers of the poker rooms you play in, so you can get the jackpot information whenever you want.

POKER & HOLD'EM ODDS

With a deck of fifty-two cards and no wilds, there are exactly 2,598,960 different five-card hands that can be made. The ranking of poker hands is based on one fact only–how difficult it is to be dealt that hand in exactly five cards. The more difficult it is to be dealt a particular poker hand in five cards, the higher that hand ranks on the scale of poker hands. Here's a list of how those poker hands break down:

Poker Hand	Odds Against	Example
Royal Flush	649,739 to 1	A♠ K♠ Q♠ J♠ 10♠
Straight Flush	64,973 to 1	9♥ 8♥ 7♥ 6♥ 5♥
Four of a Kind	4,164 to 1	8♥ 8♦ 8♣ 8♠ Q♣
Full House	693 to 1	K♣ K♥ K♦ 9♠ 9♣
Flush	508 to 1	A♦ J♦ 9♦ 7♦ 3♦
Straight	254 to 1	Q♦ J♥ 10♣ 9♠ 8♥
Three of a Kind	46 to 1	7♠ 7♣ 7♥ K♦ 2♥
Two Pair	20 to 1	A♥ A♦ 7♦ 7♠ J♣
One Pair	1.25 to 1	9♥ 9♣ A♠ 8♦ 2♥
No Pair	1.002 to 1	A♥ 10♣ 9♠ 6♦ 3♥

The only games where these odds apply directly are 5-card stud and Caribbean stud, which are games where you are dealt exactly five cards with no opportunity to draw or exchange cards. Although, as you'll see, the odds are not the same for seven-card games like Texas hold'em or 7-card stud, the ranks of the hands do not change order.

The above list of ranks of poker hands is the one thing that all forms of poker have in common. Even games that are played for low (where the lowest hand wins) use this list. The only difference is that the best hand is determined by starting at the bottom of the list and working up. Since this book is intended for beginners, I'm not going to get into the complicated math used to arrive at the above figures. It's important, though, that you understand the math that applies specifically to Texas hold'em.

Math for Texas hold'em players breaks down into five separate categories:

1. Preflop Odds
2. Odds for the Flop
3. Odds for the Turn
4. Odds for the River
5. Pot Odds

Preflop odds cover everything that you can know about any combination of two cards. Odds for the flop tell you what you can expect with those two cards when you add three more cards on the flop. Odds for the turn tell you what you can know in advance about that single turn card and how it affects your hand. Odds for the river are similar to odds for the turn, because each card comes one at a time and you will usually be looking for one of them to complete your draw. Pot odds concern the amount of money in the pot and how that relates to your drawing odds. We'll cover pot odds in a later chapter.

Preflop Odds

There are exactly 1,326 different ways you can be dealt any two cards in the deck. The odds of dealing any card you name off the top of the deck are one in fifty-two. The odds of dealing the next card you name are one in fifty-one. 52 x 51 = 2,652. Since these two cards can come in either order, you divide by two, which gives you 1,326.

1,326 is a very important number for a hold'em player. You have to commit it to memory if you plan to do some of the math it takes to win at hold'em. Many of the decisions you're going to have to make in a hold'em game start with knowing this number.

There are only six ways to be dealt each pair. Since you have only four cards of each rank to work with when creating pairs, there are only six possible combinations:

1. ♠ ♣   2. ♠ ♥   3. ♠ ♦
4. ♣ ♥   5. ♣ ♦   6. ♥ ♦

If you don't understand this calculation, or if you think six combinations is too small a number, I'd like you to see it for yourself. Remove the four cards of any rank from a deck and see how many ways you can combine them. You'll see that the only possible combinations are spade/club, spade/heart, spade/diamond, club/heart, club/diamond, and heart/diamond, just as listed above. That's six combinations.

Any two cards that are not a pair (let's use AK as an example) can come in sixteen different combinations. The A♥ can combine with each of the four different kings, as can the A♦, the A♣, and the A♠. Four aces combining with four kings makes sixteen possible combinations. Here they are:

1.	A♠ K♠	2.	A♠ K♣
3.	A♠ K♥	4.	A♠ K♦
5.	A♣ K♠	6.	A♣ K♣
7.	A♣ K♥	8.	A♣ K♦
9.	A♥ K♠	10.	A♥ K♣
11.	A♥ K♥	12.	A♥ K♦
13.	A♦ K♠	14.	A♦ K♣
15.	A♦ K♥	16.	A♦ K♦

Four of these combinations are suited. This will be true of all unpaired hand combinations so, since 16/4 = 4, you may correctly deduce that one-fourth of all unpaired, two-card hands will be suited.

Already, without having worked that hard, you know four things:

POKER & HOLD'EM ODDS

1. There are 1,326 different hold'em hands.
2. There are only six ways to make a pair.
3. There are sixteen ways to make an unpaired hand.
4. One-fourth of unpaired hands are suited.

If you compare these facts with each other and apply your card sense, there are a few other facts that you can probably deduce:

5. If you disregard suits, there are 169 different possible two-card hands. Any one of the thirteen ranks can combine with any one of the other thirteen ranks (13 x 13 = 169) to make a hand.

6. Of the 1,326 total hands, seventy-eight of them are pairs (13 ranks x 6 combinations = 78 different pairs).

7. Since #6 above is true, one out of every seventeen hands you're dealt will be a pair (1,326/78 = 17).

8. Since #7 above is true, the odds of being dealt any pair you specify (it's usually aces) are one out of 221. If someone asks you, "What're the odds of being dealt pocket aces on the next hand?" you can confidently answer, "220 to 1." Another way to check this answer is to divide the six ways to make pocket aces into the 1,326 possible hands (1,326/6 = 221).

9. If you have absolutely no information about a player's hand, you know that odds are sixteen to six (or eight to three) that he does not hold a pocket pair.

The unpaired hand is two and two-thirds more likely than the pair (6 x 2 2/3 = 16).

Odds for the Flop

1. When you hold two cards out of the deck, there are exactly 19,600 different flops that can come up. This means that the odds of flopping any three exact cards you name are 15,999 to 1.

2. If you hold a pocket pair, you will flop four of a kind .245% (.00245) of the time. Odds: 407.16 to 1.

3. If you hold a pocket pair, you'll flop a full house .980% of the time. Odds: 101.04 to 1. One-fourth of the time, however, the set (three of a kind) will be on the board, so your full house won't be well disguised.

4. If you hold a pocket pair, you will flop four to a straight 2.612% of the time. Odds: 37.28 to 1.

5. If you hold a pocket pair, you will flop another pair 16.163% of the time. Odds: 5.18 to 1.

6. When your hand is not a pair, you will flop four of a kind .000102% of the time. Odds: 9,802.92 to 1. Actually, there are only two flops out of 19,600 that will give you four of a kind. For example, if you held A♥ K♥, only one flop would be the other three aces and only one flop would be the other three kings.

7. When your hand is not a pair, you will flop a full house .092% of the time. Odds: 1,085.95 to 1.

8. When your hand is not a pair, you will flop a straight anywhere between .327% and 1.306% of the time depending on whether you hold AK (where only a 10, jack and queen will help you) or 98 (where flops of QJ10, J107, 1076, and 765 will help you. Odds: 304.81 to 1 and 75.56 to 1.

9. When your hand is not a pair, you will flop three of a kind 1.57% of the time. Odds: 62.69 to 1. One-seventh of the time, though, the three of a kind will be on the board. So, when you hold a hand like K♦ J♥, you'll get two more kings or jacks on the flop 1.347% of the time (6/7 of 1.57%). Odds: 53.59 to 1.

10. When your hand is not a pair, you will flop two pair 4.014% of the time. Odds: 23.91 to 1. Exactly one-half of the time, however, one of the pairs will be on the board.

11. When your hand is not a pair, you will flop one pair 40.408% of the time. Odds: 1.47 to 1. One-third of these pairs, however, will be on the board and not paired with one of your hole cards. That means that you will flop a pair with one of your hole cards 26.939% of the time. Odds: 2.71 to 1.

12. When your hole cards are suited, you will flop a flush .837% of the time. Odds: 118.47 to 1.

13. When your hole cards are suited, you will flop a four-flush 10.944% of the time. Odds: 8.13 to 1.

14. When your hole cards are not suited, you will flop a four-flush 2.245% of the time. Odds: 43.54 to 1.

Overcards on the Flop

An overcard is a card on the flop that is higher than the highest card in your hand. It's important because it represents the threat that it has paired one of your opponent's hole cards. If you hold 9♥ 9♣ and the flop is K♣ 8♠ 3♦, then the K♣ is the overcard to your hand.

You must hold an ace not to worry about an overcard on the flop. That happens only 14.9% of the time.

Percent Chance That You Will Flop an Overcard						
You Hold	None	One	Two	Three	One or More	An Overcard and No Set if Paired
K♣K♦ or KX	77.449	21.122	1.408	0.020	22.550	11.67
Q♦Q♥ or QX	58.571	35.143	6.000	0.286	41.429	31.12
J♥J♠ or JX	43.041	43.041	12.796	1.122	56.959	46.96
10♠10♣ or TX	30.531	45.796	20.816	2.875	69.487	59.57
9♣9♦ or 9X	20.714	44.388	29.082	5.816	79.286	69.30
8♦8♥ or 8X	13.265	39.796	36.612	10.327	86.735	76.54
7♥7♠ or 7X	7.857	33.000	42.429	16.714	92.143	81.65
6♠6♣ or 6X	4.163	24.980	45.551	25.306	95.837	85.01
5♣5♦ or 5X	1.857	16.714	45.000	36.429	98.143	86.97
4♦4♥ or 4X	0.612	9.184	39.796	50.408	99.388	87.92
3♥3♠ or 3X	0.102	3.367	28.959	67.571	99.898	88.22
2♠2♣ or 2X	impossible	0.245	11.510	88.245	100.000	88.24

In the above chart, the headings "None," "One," "Two," and "Three" mean the chance of having exactly that many overcards come on the flop. For example, if you hold Q♥ Q♣, there will be exactly two overcards (aces or kings) on the flop 6.0% of the time.

The "One or More" column is the total of the One, Two, and Three columns. The last column gives the odds of getting at least one overcard without flopping a set when you hold a pair. In other words, if you hold a pocket pair, it gives the odds you won't like the flop.

The following table shows you what to expect when you don't have suited cards and aren't looking to make a straight, either. If you're hoping to pair the highest card in your hand on the flop, this table is for you.

CHANCES OF FLOPPING THE TOP PAIR

If you hold an unpaired	% chance it will be the highest card on the flop
A	16.6
K	13.9
Q	11.3
J	9.1
10	7.1
9	5.4
8	3.9
7	2.6
6	1.6
5	0.8
4	0.3
3	0.1
2	0.0

There's something else that's useful to know: how your pocket cards compare to the other players' cards before the flop. If you know all the possible two-card combinations (1,326) and you know how many other players are dealt into the hand, you can compute the chance that you have the best hand before the flop. I've done that for you—take a look at the table on the next page.

POKER & HOLD'EM ODDS

Odds That Someone Holds a Better Hand Than You Preflop

You hold	Odds that someone else holds	# of players in the hand		
		8	9	10
K♣K♦	A♥A♠	24.6-1	21.8-1	19.5-1
A♦K♥	A♠A♥, K♠K♣	24.8-1	21.9-1	19.7-1
Q♦Q♣	A♥A♠, K♣K♠	12.0-1	10.6-1	9.5-1
J♣J♦	A♠A♦, K♥K♠, Q♦Q♥	7.9-1	6.9-1	6.2-1
10♠10♥	A♣A♦, K♦K♥, Q♠Q♣, J♥J♦	5.8-1	5.1-1	4.5-1
A♥Q♠	A♣A♦, K♥K♠, A♥K♦, Q♣Q♠	5.7-1	5.0-1	4.4-1
9♥9♦	A♣A♦, K♥K♠, Q♦Q♥, J♠J♣, 10♣10♦	4.5-1	4.0-1	3.5-1
K♠Q♥	A♣A♦, K♥K♠, Q♦Q♥, A♣K♦, A♦Q♠	3.6-1	3.1-1	2.7-1
A♥J♠	A♣A♦, K♥K♠, Q♦Q♥, J♠J♣, A♦K♣, A♥Q♣	3.0-1	2.6-1	2.3-1
K♦J♠	A♣A♦, K♥K♠, Q♠Q♥, J♦J♣, A♦K♥, A♣J♥, K♠Q♥	2.2-1	1.9-1	1.7-1
A♥10♦	A♣A♦, K♥K♠, Q♦Q♥, J♠J♣, 10♥10♣, A♦K♥, A♠Q♠, A♥J♣	1.9-1	1.7-1	1.4-1
Q♥J♣	A♣A♦, K♥K♠, Q♦Q♥, J♣J♠, A♦Q♣, A♠J♣, K♥Q♥, K♦J♣	1.7-1	1.5-1	1.3-1
K♠10♦	A♣A♦, K♥K♠, Q♦Q♥, J♣J♥, 10♥10♦, A♥K♣, A♠10♣, K♥Q♦, K♣J♠	1.5-1	1.3-1	1.1-1
A♦9♥	A♣A♦, K♥K♠, Q♦Q♥, J♣J♠, 10♥10♦, 9♠9♦, A♣K♦, A♥Q♠, A♣J♠, A♥10♦	1.4-1	1.2-1	50.2%
Q♠10♥	A♣A♦, K♥K♠, Q♣Q♠, J♦J♥, 10♠10♦, A♥Q♦, A♣10♠, K♥Q♦, K♠10♦, Q♣J♥	1.2-1	1.0-1	52.9%
K♥9♦	A♣A♦, K♥K♠, Q♦Q♥, J♠J♣, 10♦10♥, 9♥9♦, A♠K♥, A♥9♦, K♦Q♠, K♣J♦, K♥10♠	1.1-1	51.5%	55.5%

Odds for the Turn

There are two types of hands in hold'em:

1. A pair or better.
2. A draw to a straight or flush.

Every hand that is played after the flop is a contest between these two types of hands or within each type of hand. Classic examples would be:

1. One player has flopped top pair with a good kicker, while his opponent has flopped a straight or a flush draw:

You Hold	The Flop is	I Hold
A♠ K♣	K♥ 7♦ 6♣	8♠ 9♣
Q♥ J♣	J♦ 8♦ 3♥	6♦ 5♦

2. Both players have flopped the same pair, but one player is ahead of the other because he has a better kicker:

You Hold	The Flop is	I Hold
A♥ 9♣	9♠ K♣ 5♥	10♥ 9♦

3. Both players have flopped a straight draw, but one player has higher cards than the other:

You Hold	The Flop is	I Hold
K♣ Q♣	J♦ 9♥ 8♣	7♠ 6♠

4. Both players have flopped a flush draw, but one player has higher cards than the other:

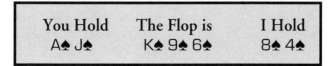

You Hold	The Flop is	I Hold
A♠ J♠	K♠ 9♠ 6♠	8♠ 4♠

5. Both players started with mediocre hands, and they both totally missed the flop:

You Hold	The Flop is	I Hold
J♥ 5♦	A♣ 9♠ 2♦	7♦ 3♥

In all of the examples above, there's an easy way to figure out how each hand will turn out. All you have to do is determine how many outs you have and compute the chances of hitting your outs on the turn and the river. I've done this for you in the table on the next page.

Drawing Odds From a Deck of 47 Unseen Cards

Number of outs	2 Cards to come	1 Card to come	Example
20	67.5%	43.5%	
19	65.0%	41.3%	
18	62.4%	39.1%	
17	59.8%	37.0%	
16	57.0%	34.8%	
15	54.1%	32.6%	Open-end straight flush draw
14	51.2%	30.4%	
13	48.1%	28.3%	
12	45.0%	26.1%	Flopped a four-flush and pairing a hole card wins.
11	41.7%	23.9%	
10	38.4%	21.7%	Flopped a set and missed the full house on the turn.
9	35.0%	19.6%	Flopped a four-flush
8	31.5%	17.4%	Open-end straight draw
7	27.8%	15.2%	Flopped a set, need to fill up.
6	24.1%	13.0%	
5	20.4%	10.9%	Hold A♣K♦ and flopped an ace or king.
4	16.5%	8.7%	Inside straight draw/you pair both hole cards.
3	12.5%	6.5%	Have a pair and need to hit your kicker.
2	8.4%	4.3%	Hold a pair and did not flop a set.
1	4.3%	2.2%	Need exactly one specific card to win.

If you get top pair from the flop, how likely is it that you'll get an overcard on the turn or the river?

Take a look at the table below:

CHANCE OF GETTING AN OVERCARD ON THE TURN OR RIVER AFTER YOU FLOP TOP PAIR

If your top pair is:	% of the time an overcard will come on the turn or river
A	00
K	17
Q	32
J	45
10	57
9	68
8	77
7	84
6	90
5	95
4	98
3	100

For example, if you hold 9♥ 8♣, and the three-card flop is 9♣ 7♦ 4♠, a 10, jack, queen, king, or ace will come on the turn or river 68% of the time.

Odds for the River

With one final card to come, it's very easy to compute your drawing odds. All you have to do is count how many outs you have and divide that number into the cards that you have not yet seen. When you're computing your odds after the flop (but before the turn), that number will usually be 47, unless someone has exposed a card or two in the process of mucking his hand. Again, I've done these computations for you. Look at the "1 Card to Come" column in the table on page 82.

Some Overall Percentages

We have now looked at the odds of getting various hands at all stages of hold'em. As a reference tool for you, I have also included three charts of your overall winning chances with any hand. You'll find those on the next page.

POKER & HOLD'EM ODDS

Winning Percentages for Four (4) Players
(Add 3% for suited cards)

	K	Q	J	10	9	8	7	6	5	4	3	2
A	41	39	38	37	36	34	33	31	30	29	28	27
K	-	36	35	33	31	30	28	27	26	25	24	23
Q	-	-	34	32	30	28	26	25	24	23	22	20
J	-	-	-	30	28	26	25	23	33	21	20	19
10	-	-	-	-	27	25	24	22	21	20	19	18
9	-	-	-	-	-	23	22	21	20	19	18	17
8	-	-	-	-	-	-	22	21	19	18	17	16
7	-	-	-	-	-	-	-	21	19	18	17	16
6	-	-	-	-	-	-	-	-	19	18	17	16
5	-	-	-	-	-	-	-	-	-	18	16	15
4	-	-	-	-	-	-	-	-	-	-	16	15
3	-	-	-	-	-	-	-	-	-	-	-	14

Winning Percentages for Seven (7) Players

	K	Q	J	10	9	8	7	6	5	4	3	2
A	27	25	24	23	21	20	18	17	16	15	14	13
K	-	22	21	19	18	17	16	15	14	13	12	11
Q	-	-	20	18	16	15	24	23	22	10	9	9
J	-	-	-	17	15	18	13	11	10	9	9	8
10	-	-	-	-	14	13	12	11	10	9	9	8
9	-	-	-	-	-	12	11	10	9	8	8	7
8	-	-	-	-	-	-	11	10	9	8	8	7
7	-	-	-	-	-	-	-	10	9	8	8	7
6	-	-	-	-	-	-	-	-	9	8	8	7
5	-	-	-	-	-	-	-	-	-	8	7	6
4	-	-	-	-	-	-	-	-	-	-	7	6
3	-	-	-	-	-	-	-	-	-	-	-	6

Winning Percentages for Ten (10) Players

	K	Q	J	10	9	8	7	6	5	4	3	2
A	21	19	17	16	15	14	13	12	11	10	9	8
K	-	17	15	14	13	12	11	10	9	8	8	7
Q	-	-	14	13	11	10	9	9	8	8	7	7
J	-	-	-	11	10	10	9	8	8	7	7	6
10	-	-	-	-	10	9	8	8	7	7	6	6
9	-	-	-	-	-	9	8	7	7	6	6	5
8	-	-	-	-	-	-	8	7	7	6	5	5
7	-	-	-	-	-	-	-	7	6	5	5	4
6	-	-	-	-	-	-	-	-	6	5	4	4
5	-	-	-	-	-	-	-	-	-	5	4	3
4	-	-	-	-	-	-	-	-	-	-	4	3
3	-	-	-	-	-	-	-	-	-	-	-	3

Structure Your Learning

Assignment #3

I admit that I've just given you quite a bit of statistical information, and most of it probably seems meaningless. As I promised, you do not have to memorize these tables. Your assignment is to complete the quiz that follows. Because this is an open book test–all of the answers are right here in Chapter 7—I want you to make sure to score 100%. These questions are designed to point out for you the more relevant and useful statistics that you'll need to know to be a successful hold'em player. Answers are at the end of the quiz.

1. How many different poker hands are there in a fifty-two card deck?

2. How many of those hands do not even make a pair?

3. How many two card hands can be made from a fifty-two card deck?

4. How many different ways are there to make a pair of kings (or any other pair you name)?

5. How many different ways are there to make an unpaired two-card hand?

6. What percent of unpaired two-card hands are suited?

7. If you disregard suits, how many different two-card hands are there?

8. How many different pairs are there? (Hint: It's not thirteen).

9. What are the odds of your getting a pocket pair on any one deal?

10. What is the chance you will be dealt a pair of aces on your next hand?

11. What is the chance you will be dealt a pair of kings on your next hand?

12. What is the chance that you will be dealt aces, kings, or AK on your next hand?

13. If you hold A♣ K♥, how often will you flop two more aces or two more kings?

14. How often will you flop just one of your hole cards?

15. When you start with two suited cards, how often will you flop a four-flush?

16. If you hold K♥ K♣, how often will you get one or more aces on the flop?

17. If you hold K♠ J♦, what is the chance you will flop another king with no A?

18. If you hold 9♦ 8♥, what is the chance you will flop another 9 and it will be the highest card on the flop?

19. If you hold K♣ Q♦, and the flop is K♦ J♦ 9♥, what is the chance that an ace will come on the turn or river?

20. If you hold 10♥ 9♥, and the flop is 8♥ 7♥ 4♣, what is the chance you will make a straight or a flush on the turn or the river?

21. If you hold 8♠ 8♣, and the flop is A♣ 8♥ 2♦, how many outs do you have to improve your hand on the turn? Write them down for future reference.

22. Continuing with the above question, the turn card is the 5♦. How many outs do you have to improve your hand on the river? Write them down.

23. If you flop a four-flush, how many outs do you have, and what is the chance you'll make the flush by the river?

24. If you flop an open-end straight, how many outs do you have, and what is the chance you'll make the straight by the river?

25. If you flop an inside straight-draw, how many outs do you have, and what is the chance you'll make the straight by the river?

26. If you hold 7♦ 7♥ and don't get another 7 on the flop, what are the odds that you'll get one by the river?

27. If you hold K♥ K♣, what are the odds that someone else holds pocket aces before the flop in a ten-handed game?

28. If you hold 10♣ 10♠, what are the odds that someone holds a higher pocket pair before the flop in a ten-handed game?

29. If you hold A♥ 9♥, what are the odds that someone holds a better hand than you do before the flop in a ten-handed game?

30. How often will A♣ K♠ be the winning hand in a ten-handed game?

CARDOZA PUBLISHING • WARREN

Answers to Assignment #3

1. 2,598,960

2. one-half

3. 1,326

4. 6

5. 16

6. 25%

7. 169

8. 78

9. 16-1

10. 220-1

11. 220-1. It's 220-1 for any pair you specify.

12. 6 + 6 + 16 = 28 total hands. 1,326 divided by 28 = 47.35. That makes odds of 46.35 to 1.

13. 1.347% of the time, or odds of 53.59 to 1.

14. 26.939% of the time, or odds of 2.71 to 1.

15. 10.944% of the time, or odds of 8.13 to 1.

16. 22.55% of the time.

17. 13.9%

18. 5.4%

19. 17%

20. 54.1%

21. 7. They are A♠, A♦, A♥, 8♦, 2♣, 2♥, and 2♠.

22. 10. Adding the 5♦ adds the 5♥, 5♣ and the 5♠ to your possible outs.

23. 9, 35%

24. 8, 31.5%

25. 4, 16.5%

26. 8.4%

27. 19.5-1

28. 4.5-1

29. 50.2%, or 1 to 1

30. 21%. 24% if the AK were suited.

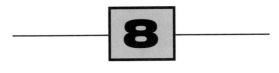

POSITION

Position is a very important concept to consider when playing poker. It's especially important when playing flop games like hold'em and Omaha because your betting position stays the same throughout all four betting rounds of the hand. If you're first to bet before the flop, then you'll be first to bet on the flop, on the turn, and on the river. You will always have to make your move without knowing what the players behind you will do, while the other players will always be able to decide how to play their hands in light of what you've already done.

Your position relative to the other players is so important that it's one factor you'll have to consider when deciding to play every hand that you're going to play for the rest of your poker-playing life. Here's a good rule: play extremely tight **under the gun** (in first position), tight in early position, and add a few more hands to your playable list only as your position improves. Your position improves as players ahead of you act on their hands. Your position also gets better from one betting round to the next as players behind you fold.

Usually, your main objective is to play your hand for one bet (to see the flop), hoping that no one left to act on his hand raises you, thereby making you have to fold or see the flop for two bets when your hand is worth only one bet. A raise behind you also opens up the possibility that someone who previously called ahead of you will now reraise.

When you call to see the flop, there are a few things you should consider. First, you should estimate whether you can see the flop for just one bet. You can never know for sure so don't be upset if you are occasionally raised. How many players are left to act behind you? The more there are, the more likely it is you could be raised. Exactly what is your hand? Is it good enough to play for two bets when you'd rather play it for one bet?

There's another drawback to being in early position: it's a little harder to bluff and represent good hands when you have to play early. Consider this hand as an example: you have A♠ K♥ in early position and you raise, making it two bets to go. Everyone folds around to the button, who raises again, making it three bets. Everyone folds around to you and you decide to put in the last raise, hoping to give the impression that you could have A♣ A♥ or K♦ K♥. It's just the two of you to see the flop. The flop is 4♣ 7♥ 4♦, which misses you completely. You feel that it could also have missed your sole opponent, so you bet on the flop to give him a chance to fold. Instead, he raises you!

POSITION

This raise probably means one of two things:

1. He knows he has a better hand than yours and he wants to make you pay to beat him.

2. He wants to intimidate you so you'll check on the turn, when the bets double.

You just call and see the turn card. The turn is the 8♠, missing you again. You've decided, though, that the raise on the flop was meant to slow you down. Since you're a good player and you know that it's usually a good idea to do the opposite of what the other players want you to do, you go ahead and bet on the turn. Again, your sole opponent calls you. Calling a big bet on the turn after raising before the flop and on the flop usually means you have a big pocket pair, particularly when the board has only low cards, as is the case here.

The river card is the Q♣. Because of the way your opponent has played his hand you have to guess he has A♥ A♣, K♣ K♦, or Q♥ Q♦. You have to check. When you do, he bets, and you reluctantly have to fold. What do you think he had? I'll tell you. It was A♣ K♦, the same hand you had! So why didn't you split the pot, since you had the same hand? It's because your opponent had *position* on you. This exact situation arises frequently in hold'em, and because of the community card aspect of the game and the obvious benefits of being in late position, it's hard to win hands when playing from an early position.

Here's another common example. You have J♦ 8♦, and the flop is 9♥ 7♣ 5♠. A 10 or a 6 will make you a straight. You check and call. The turn is the Q♠. Again, you check and call. The river is the 2♣. You missed. This time you have to check, and when your sole opponent bets, you have to fold. What did he have? Would you be surprised if I told you he had the same hand you did? How about if I told you he had 4♥ 3♦, a hand you could obviously have beaten? The point is it doesn't matter what cards he had. The important thing he had was *position*. These two examples illustrate why you usually should not play purely drawing hands from an early position.

9

STARTING HANDS

Most poker writers have their own idea of what constitutes a group of good starting hands. In my first
book, *The Winner's Guide to Texas Hold'em Poker*, I
gave one list of starting hands. For our purposes here,
we're going to use the list below, which I've created
specifically for this book.

> **GROUP 1**: AA, KK, QQ, AKs*, AQs
> **GROUP 2**: JJ, 1010, AJs, KQs, AK
> **GROUP 3**: A10s, KJs, QJs, J10s, AQ
> **GROUP 4**: 99, 88, K10s, Q10s, J9s, 109s, 98s, AJ, KQ
> *"s" represents "suited"

The hands are arranged in these groups because each
hand in a group has approximately the same value to
you before the flop as the other hands listed in the
group. That means that before the flop, all hands in a
group can be played in about the same way. Of course,
each hand will be played differently after the flop, so
keep in mind that this guide applies before the flop
only. Knowing this list and following the advice I will

give you about how to play these hands will help keep you out of trouble while you're learning the other aspects of the game.

Structure Your Learning

Assignment #4

Memorize Groups 1, 2, and 3 of my starting hands. This list is designed specifically to thwart higher limit players and good lower limit players who know how to take advantage of you if you're playing too loose for your position. Following this list will help ensure that you're in a good position for the hands you play so you'll have a decent chance to win them.

Assignment #5

1. Next time you play hold'em in your regular game, always raise and reraise with Group 1 hands. When you have these hands, be the one to put in the last raise before the flop.

2. With Group 2 hands, always raise before the flop, if you are first after the big blind to enter the pot. If you are reraised, just call.

3. With Group 3 hands, always see the flop, unless you have to call three or four bets cold. If you call two bets cold and a player behind you reraises, go ahead and call to see the flop.

4. Play Group 4 hands if you can limp in for only one bet. Don't call two or more bets cold, but if you

limp in for one bet and someone raises behind you, go ahead and call to see the flop.

5. Do not play any other hand unless you are in one of the blinds.

6. Make a list of Groups 1, 2, 3, and 4 and jot down how I'm asking you to play the hands in those groups. You can take this list with you to the game and refer to it as you like.

7. Calculate how many hands there are in each of the first four groups and determine what percentage of all possible hands this represents.

8. Play as many times as you like using the above instructions. Once you understand and can manage at the table without referring to any notes, you can leave your list at home.

9. Don't forget to keep detailed records of your playing sessions, as you learned to do in Chapter 4.

ANOTHER STRATEGY FOR PREFLOP PLAY

I hope you successfully accomplished the assignment in the last chapter. If you memorized the groups of starting hands, and you followed the advice about calling and raising, you should have had good results, considering your level of experience and understanding of the game. Even if you were not a big winner, you should have noticed a few things about the games you were in.

You might have noticed that you were playing fewer hands than most of the other players in the game. You might also have noticed that you threw away a lot of hands before the flop that would have been winners. Maybe you realized that when you were in a hand, your cards were probably higher than your opponents' hands, on average. When you all missed your hands, you probably won the pot with ace-high a few times. Finally, you might also have realized that the other players respected your play, and they didn't try to run over you too much.

There are twenty-six hands in Group 1, thirty-two hands in Group 2, twenty-eight hands in Group 3, and fifty-six hands in Group 4. This adds up to 142 total hands, which is 10.71% of all possible hands. That means that you were playing about one out of every eight hands, not counting the blinds. That's pretty tight play for your average low limit game. My main purpose in having you play this tight is to allow you to sit in the game and learn it without being exposed to large fluctuations in your bankroll.

The other purpose of having you play this tight is to show you how a high limit player or semi-pro would play before the flop. This style of play is called tight/aggressive, and it usually works very well in any hold'em game. It's not the most profitable style of play at all times in all games, but it is a great way to start when you're first learning the game.

In the long run, if you're a good enough player, any profit you make will come from the mistakes your opponents make when they play against you. One typical mistake your opponents will make is to play too many hands. Poker theory says that the best way for you to take advantage of that error is also to play a few more hands than average. Don't play too many more hands, though, just a few more.

I'm now going to show you another starting hand strategy. This new strategy is designed to be fairly conservative, safe, easy-to-understand, a little more fun to play, and, most importantly, a little more profitable than the other strategy you learned in the last chapter. Another advantage you'll have is that once you've learned this new strategy, you will then know two different starting hand strategies, so you'll have options when playing before the flop. You won't always play the same way with the same cards, so your opponents won't always be sure of what you have, which increases the likelihood that they'll make mistakes. Remember, your opponents' mistakes mean more profit for you.

The new way of choosing your starting hands that you're about to learn is pretty easy because it's based on understanding your play rather than memorizing certain groups of hands. Let's take a look at your second strategy for playing before the flop.

For the most part, you're going to consider playing with these three types of hands:

1. **Pocket Pairs.** You can now play virtually all pocket pairs. You can even see the flop with the small pairs under the right conditions, as I'll explain in a moment.

2. **Suited Aces.** Hands like A♠ 8♠ or even A♠ 2♠ qualify under this category.

3. **Hands that add up to 20 or 21.** An ace counts as 11, face cards count as 10, and all other cards are worth their face value. For example, AJ is 21 points, KQ is 20 points, and A9 is 20 points. A♠ 8♣ is not a playable hand because it is not suited and does not add up to twenty.

There are forty-eight pocket pairs below a pair of 10s (pairs of 10 and above fall in the third category). There are twenty-eight hands that are suited aces that do not add up to 20 or 21, and there are 206 hands that add up to 20 or 21. This total constitutes 21.3% of all possible hands. That's twice as many hands as you were playing using the other system.

Not all of these hands are playable all the time from all positions. There are several factors that you have to consider when deciding whether to see the flop with your hand. I'm going to run down the list with some general advice about how to play each hand.

1. Pocket Pairs

AA - This is the best hand you can get before the flop. It's the hand that wins more often than any other hand, and it's the hand that wins the most money for you in the long run. Put another way, you could not do better than to have pocket aces every hand for the rest of your poker playing life. If you did, you wouldn't have to read the rest of this (or any other) poker book!

There are several ways to play pocket aces before the flop. Which strategy you choose depends on which goal you want to focus on. If you raise in early position, you will knock out most players, which will increase your chances of winning the hand. Since there will be only a few players in the hand, however, a raise in early position will also decrease the size of the final pot. If you are in late position, and a lot of players have already called, your raise will build a big pot, but the presence of so many players in the pot reduces your chances of winning the hand. It's a trade-off between small pot with a good chance of winning and a large pot with a reduced chance of winning the hand.

If you're in early position with pocket aces, you can also just call and hope that someone behind you will raise. Then you can backraise. You'll build a pot, and, if there are a few players between you and the raiser, you might knock someone out of the hand. This play builds the pot, possibly increases your chances of winning the hand, and gets some dead money in the pot. All of these benefits are very good for you.

KK - You can play pocket kings in almost the same way you play pocket aces, but you have to consider a few more things. Even though the odds are 19.5 to 1 against it, any other player who's raising could have pocket aces. There's also the dreaded ace overcard on the flop, which will come 22.5% of the time. For these reasons, if you're in late position with pocket kings, you might want to just limp in for one bet to see the flop. If you get an ace on the flop, it's easier to throw the hand away, since you have only one bet invested. Plus, if you flop another king or something else you really like, your strength will be very well disguised.

QQ - You will flop one or more overcards without another queen on the board 31.1% of the time. If there are a lot of players already in the pot, you're not going to knock anyone out by raising. If six players have already called, then they have a total of twelve cards among them. It's very likely that's there's an ace and a king among those twelve cards, so I generally do not raise in late position with pocket queens. I like to limp in for one bet. If an ace or a king comes on the flop and there's a bet, I can easily throw the hand away.

I want to emphasize that you're not really playing against just the one player who bet. You're playing against those twelve cards the others are holding. If you're not sure you understand what I mean, try this quick and easy exercise:

Pull two queens from a full deck of cards. Shuffle the rest of the cards well, and then look at the first twelve cards off the top of the deck. Is there an ace or a king in those cards? I just performed this exercise twenty times and there was an ace or a king nineteen out of those twenty times. I don't know if twenty trials is a large enough sample to be statistically valid, but it's good enough for me, particularly since this nineteen out of twenty seems to coincide with my actual experiences in years of play. Kings and aces among these cards suggest that at least one of those players who just called may have an overcard to your queen.

JJ - You will get an overcard and no jack 47% of the time. For that reason, I usually like to see the flop as cheaply as possible, because I know that I'll often be throwing it away often after the flop. There are two exceptions. If I'm in late position and only the blinds are in, I will raise to steal the blinds. If everyone has called and it's raised, I will reraise to build a pot, since

I have great drawing odds.

1010 - The best advice I can give you is to play this hand even more carefully than you play pocket jacks. You will get an overcard and no 10 60% of the time. If there's no overcard on the flop, one will come on the turn or river 57% of the time. You usually have to flop another 10 or be drawing to the high end of a straight to have a good hand after the flop with pocket 10s.

99, 88, 77, 66, 55, 44, 33, 22 - I put all of these pairs in the same category because each one has an incredibly high probability of flopping an overcard without flopping a set. The lower your pocket pair is, the more all caveats apply, and the luckier you have to get on the flop. If you stay in, see the flop as cheaply as you can. There's no law that says you have to play the hand anyway. I routinely fold pocket 2s, 3s, 4s, and 5s if it's raised preflop and I respect the raiser. You can raise to steal the blinds in late position with these hands, but your decision to do so should depend on your ability to play and read your opponent after the flop, if he calls.

2. Suited Aces

AKs - I play this hand before the flop about the same way I play pocket aces, kings or queens. You will flop an ace, a king, a straight, a straight-draw, a flush or a four-flush about 50% of the time. With odds like that, I like to have as many players in as possible with as many raises as we can get in before the flop.

AQs, AJs, A10s - These hands play similarly to AKs, except you have to worry about the gap between the cards. With AQs, beware of a king on the flop with no ace. With AJs, watch out for a king or a queen on the flop with no ace. With A10s, a king, queen, or jack with no ace (unless, of course, it's all three) causes you concern if there's any action after the flop. The main strength of these hands is that they play very well when your opponents also have an ace with weaker kickers. You make a lot of money from players who are unlucky and have the same flush draw as you do.

A9s down to A2s - Until I see the flop, I play these hands as if they weren't suited for two good reasons:

1. If you flop an ace, your kicker is usually no good unless you make two pair with it.

2. When you have two suited cards, you'll end up without a flush about 95% of the time.

So, most of the time, you'll be stuck with the strength of your non-ace card to help win the pot, and low cards aren't usually very helpful.

3. Hands that Total 20 or 21

KQs - This hand is almost as good as AK suited, but look out for an ace on the flop. One out of three times that you make a flush with this hand, the ace of your suit will be on the board. I often don't mind getting an ace on the flop, because if a jack or 10 comes with it,

I have the nut straight-draw. It traps anyone holding an ace if you make the straight.

KJs, K10s - With these hands, you'd rather pair the jack and 10, because a pair of 10s with a king kicker is a better hand than a pair of kings with a 10 kicker (given that most hands will come down to a contest of kickers, and whatever you pair on the board might also pair your opponents' hands). Until you see the flop, you should usually play these hands as if they weren't suited, unless you're raising to steal the blinds.

QJs, Q10s, J10s - These hands do best when played against a large field or against a single opponent. If you make a straight with one of these hands, it will usually be the nut straight. You'd therefore like to have all the other players putting money into this pot that you're going to win. If you have one of these hands and you flop only top pair, then you'd like to play the hand against only one player, where you have the best chance of winning the hand.

AK - Popular poker wisdom says to raise before the flop with this hand, but my years of experience at the table and on the computer have convinced me that you should usually just limp in. The exceptions are if you're in late position and can raise in an attempt to steal the blinds, or if the game is short-handed and you can raise to knock players out. You won't flop another ace or king about 75% of the time.

If you raise before the flop and then miss, you'll often be in a position where you really don't know how to play on the flop. I recommend you think carefully about raising before the flop and don't do that to yourself if you're a beginning player. You should, however, occasionally raise with AK in late position, just as you would with pocket queens or jacks. It'll help you throw off your more observant opponents. If you get a good flop, great! You'll have gotten in an extra bet with a winning hand.

If you miss, you'll still find that the other players will often check to you, since you raised before the flop. You can surprise them by checking also and seeing the turn card for free. Sometimes they will even check around to you again, assuming that *now* you'll bet, since you showed strength before the flop, and the bets have doubled. You can check again and see the river card–and therefore the entire hand–for free. Do you see how one little raise before the flop set up all these advantages?

There's another move you can make with AK before the flop that I consider to be an expert play: throw the hand away if you have to call three or four bets cold with it. Surprised? It's only an ace and a king, and you're going to miss the flop three out of four times anyway. When you do hit the flop, you'll usually have only a pair of aces or kings. Meanwhile, what do you think the raise and reraise ahead of you before the flop meant? One of the raisers probably has pocket aces or kings. If that's true, you'll win this hand only about 3% of the time, and you'll have to play all the way to the river to do so. This situation doesn't occur that often, but it's worth mentioning because you can lose a lot of money if you're not aware of it.

AQ, AJ, A10 - Just like when these hands are suited, you have to be aware of the gaps between your cards. Nonetheless, these are good hands, especially when played against just a few opponents. If you hold A10, you will have the best hand before the flop only about 60% of the time, so you should usually see the flop as cheaply as possible.

KQ, KJ, K10, QJ, Q10, J10 - With these hands, limp in to see the flop if you can. If it is raised or reraised, you'll have to use your poker sense to figure out if you're beat before the flop. If you hold J10, odds are only 50-50 that you have the best hand before the flop (that no other player in the game holds AA, KK, QQ, JJ, 1010, AK, AQ, AJ, A10, KQ, KJ, K10, QJ, Q10 or J10 suited).

These aren't the only hands you'll ever play in hold'em. You're going to be in the blinds about 20% of the time, and most of the hands you get in the blinds (and will have to play) will be garbage. I'll cover those hands in a later chapter.

Structure Your Learning
Assignment #6

Recall which hands you voluntarily entered the pot with from Groups 1, 2, 3, and 4 in the previous chapter. Now compare that list to the new list you learned in this chapter. Determine which hands are on the new list and not on the old list. Write these new, additional hands on a piece of paper and take it with you the next time you play in your usual hold'em game.

Whenever you play one of the new hands, try to keep track of how much money you invest in the hand, and how much of the pot is profit when you win a hand. For example, if you win a $50 pot, but $12 of it was your money to begin with, count only the $38 difference as profit. If you do this long enough to get a large sample, you'll see that some of these hands will be winners and, of course, some will be losers. You can then use this list you've created to further refine your list of starting hands. If you like, you can stop playing the hands with which you often lose.

Between the groups of starting hands mentioned in the previous chapter and your new, refined list of starting hands from this chapter, you should have settled into a preflop style of play that suits you very well. Good luck.

CHOOSING A GAME AND A SEAT

Of all the things that a hold'em player can do to improve his hourly rate, one of the easiest is to give some thought to which game to play in and which seat to take at that table. Picking the right seat in the right game for you can actually mean the difference between winning and losing for that playing session.

Poker Room Selection

If you're lucky enough to have more than one poker room or casino that you can play in frequently, you should take the time to consider which one may be the most profitable for you. Some differences between poker rooms are:

1. *Distance from your home.* Is the poker room so far away that the extra driving time, both to and from the game, substantially cuts into your playing time? You may decide that the extra time is not worth it and choose to play in a poker room closer to your house.

2. *Variety and limits of games offered.* The more games they offer that you like, the better for you. When you arrive to play at a room with many games you like, there's a good chance you can get in the game you want sooner. If you do have to wait, there's also a good chance you can play your second choice game while you're moving up the list for the game you prefer.

Often, when there are more than two poker rooms in a city, one of the poker room managers will decide that he wants to differentiate his poker room by spreading games that are not offered in the other poker rooms. If you like to play very high limit or an unusual game like Pineapple hold'em, look around, because there might be a room for you.

3. *Jackpots.* Some poker rooms don't have a bad beat jackpot. Among those that do, the requirements to hit the jackpot vary. The jackpot may be very easy or very difficult to hit, depending on the rules. The rules determine the odds that the jackpot will be hit, which in turn determine how often there will be a jackpot payout (and thus how big the payouts will be). I've played in poker rooms where the jackpot was so easy to hit that it never got bigger than a few thousand dollars and was hit once or more every week.

I've also played in poker rooms where the jackpot requirements were exceedingly high. I played in one room where the requirement was that four of a kind must lose to a higher four of a kind, both hole cards in both players' hands must play, and they must beat the board. The jackpot in that poker room was more than $100,000, and it had not been hit in more than three years when it finally was hit. We'll discuss jackpots further in a later chapter.

4. Comps. Some poker rooms will give you a free meal if you play for three hours or more. The Ameristar Casino poker room in Kansas City, where I currently play, offers you credit toward any of the casino restaurants for each hour you play. If those sort of comps appeal to you, you may want to consider which ones a casino offers when choosing your poker room.

Game Selection

If a poker room has more than one game of the same limit, it's worth your time to compare the two games and decide which one you'd rather play in. An intelligent decision here requires that you first gather a little information. Take some time to watch all the games that you're considering. You're mainly looking to answer two questions:

1. How many players, on average, enter the pot to see the flop each hand?

2. How often does someone raise before the flop?

Watching a round or two ought to give you enough to go on.

A poker game may be classified from very tight to very loose, depending on how many players see the flop. If you see a game where there are only two or three players playing every hand in a full game, you know it's a very tight game. Alternatively, if everybody calls to see the flop every time, you're watching a very loose game.

How much preflop raising there is determines whether the game is passive, aggressive, or somewhere in between. You know your personality type. Do you prefer a safer, less-action game with small pots? Or do you crave the thrill of a high-action, risky game with lots of players and big pots? Knowing how many players are playing each hand and how much raising they're doing will help you pick the game that's best for you.

There's one other factor to consider when choosing a table: do you recognize any bad players in that game? Remember, your profit in this game comes from the mistakes your opponents make. You don't have to be the best player in the game. Usually, the only thing you need is not to be the worst player in the game. Playing against just one or two bad players is all you need to show a profit in the long run.

Seat Selection
Knowledge is power. Everybody knows that. At the hold'em table, look at the actions of your opponents as their way of giving you knowledge that you can use as a weapon against them. For that reason, you'd like

certain types of players to act on their hands before you do. Those players are:

1. *Loose players*. People who play too many hands cannot possibly have a premium hand every time. When you call against these players, you'll usually have the better hand, so you'll show a profit over a period of time. When you raise, the loose player will already have one bet in the pot, and he will almost always call the raise from you. If you've got a loose player on your right, you've got him trapped.

2. *Very aggressive players*. These are not the same as loose players. While a loose player plays too many hands, a very aggressive player bets, raises and reraises too much with the fewer hands that he does play. Against such a player, you'll often be in the position of having to call two or more bets cold. This is good for you for two reasons:

    a. At least you're not in the position of having called one bet and being trapped into calling another bet when someone behind you raises. You can fold without having called any bets.

    b. If your hand is very good, you can leverage the aggressive player's raise, using it to drive out other players behind you by raising yourself. You can't do this if the aggressive player is on your left.

3. *The money*. By this I mean the player who has the most money on the table, and therefore appears to be

the biggest winner in the game. True, he could have bought all of those chips, or he could just have been lucky enough to win the biggest pot of the day. In the absence of any other information, though, you can assume he's a good player. If you spent a few minutes watching the game before you got in, you'll know what kind of player he is, and you'll be able to tell if his winnings come from luck or skill. If he's really good, you want him on your right, where he'll act on his hand before you most of the time.

I can think of two good examples that illustrate why it's beneficial to sit behind the money in a hold'em game. The first is from the 1995 movie *Sabrina*, starring Harrison Ford. He plays a multimillionaire business-man, and it's revealed near the end of the movie that, unknown to him, his chauffeur is also a millionaire. "How did *he* get to be a millionaire?" you ask. Easy. All he did was listen in on the boss's conversations while working. Then he bought and sold stock based on that information.

The other example of the benefit of playing after the money comes from the blackjack table. Sometimes you will be at the same table as a known card counter. You don't have to know anything about counting cards, and you don't have to keep track of the cards that are still in the deck. You can enjoy the game, and still win, because all you have to do is watch the card counter. When he increases his bet, you increase yours. When he lowers his bet, you lower yours. He does all the mental calculations for you. His bet reflects the result of those calculations. You get the same benefit in a hold'em game, if you play after the big winner who plays well.

Most of the information that's valuable to you comes from the players on your right. It usually doesn't help you to have to act on your hand before you know what the player on your left is going to do. In other words, how do you play against a player when you have to act before he does? This isn't a problem if he is the right type of player for you. There are three types of players you shouldn't mind having on your left:

1. *Passive Players.* You can always count on these players to play only good cards, not to raise too much before the flop unless they have premium hands, and to call too often. Additionally, these players will rarely raise when you're in the blinds, which will allow you see a lot more flops.

2. *Maniacs.* These are players who play, raise, and reraise every hand. They like to try to win with what they know are weak hands, they overbet their draws, and they almost never just call. Although you might prefer to have this player on your right, there's an advantage to having him on your left.

Since you know he'll play and bet every hand and every round, if he's on your left, you can make extensive use of check-raising when you have good hands. This helps you build the pot for those hands you expect to win.

This one tactic alone has a huge positive effect on your hourly rate, which is really what it's all about.

3. *Bluffers.* The third type of player you want on your left is the player who bluffs too much. Frequently, your proper play is to check your good hands to him to give him a chance to bluff at you, especially on the river. Assuming you're going to win the hand, your goal is to get paid off on the river. If you bet first, your frequent bluffer has to have a hand to call you with, and he'll have to fold a majority of the time. If you check to him, however, he will bluff at you more often than he'll call if you've bet first. Bluffing too often is a mistake. Give him a chance to make that mistake.

Having trouble choosing your seat? Don't worry, there's also a back-up plan for seat selection. If you genuinely do not know which is the best seat in the game, or if you can't identify which players you'd rather have on your left or right, then I recommend you sit in the third or eighth seat at the hold'em table. If you can't get the third or eighth seat, the seat on either side of those seats will work as well.

From these seats, the other players will be in your field of vision all at once. All you have to do is look up to take it all in. This is important, because it's how you spot the other players' **tells**, which are worth a lot of money to you if you know how to interpret what you see. We'll discuss tells further in a later chapter.

Structure Your Learning

Assignment #7

Next time you play in your regular game, make sure you check out the different tables and try to pick the best one for you. If the floorman has you seated at a table you don't want, tell him to put you on the table change list. Once you get in the right game, start looking for the best seat, using the criteria you learned in this chapter.

When a seat comes available, the first player in the game to inform the dealer that he wants that empty seat gets it. If possible, try to avoid making it obvious why you're changing seats. You certainly don't want to actually say out loud during the game why you're moving.

When you get home, and you're completing your notes about the game, mention the seat change, the reason you changed, and what you think the results of your move were. Make this process a regular part of your note-taking.

RAISING

Poker theory says that all betting starts out as a contest for the antes or, in the case of flop games, the blinds. When a player has no money invested in the hand, and the size of the pot is very small, he has little incentive to enter the pot unless his hand is very good. If he does call, he knows that other players behind him might also call, so he will often raise to discourage competitors from entering the pot. This play is called **raising to eliminate players**. It's only one of the five major reasons to raise, especially before the flop.

The five major reasons to raise are:

1. To eliminate players.
2. To get a free card.
3. To gain information.
4. To get value from your hand.
5. To bluff or semi-bluff.

Raising to eliminate players works best before the flop, when a player doesn't have any money invested in the pot. It also works well on the flop and on the turn, when a player may have only one bet in the pot, and he doesn't have the right odds to continue with the hand. Raising to eliminate players on the river is less effective, because at that point all the cards are out. Your opponent will call based on his pot odds and his estimation of your hand.

Raising to get a free card sometimes works before the flop, because it may induce players to check to you when they see the flop, but you can't always count on it. If the flop makes a great hand for one of your opponents, the fact that you raised before it won't stop him from betting into you. Raising to get a free card works best on the flop, when the other players flop what they consider to be weak or drawing hands. Because the bet doubles on the turn and the river, raising to get a free card doesn't work then. It costs just as much to raise as it does to call the next bet.

Raising to gain information works best if you are re-raising a before the flop raiser, or if you raise a player who has bet on the flop. Your opponent's reaction to your raise is loaded with information, if you know how to interpret what you see. You usually won't raise to gain information on the turn or on the river, because a raise there will have quite a different effect on your opponents.

Raising to get value from your hand works well before the flop, on the flop, on the turn, and on the river. A raise for value often has the undesired effect of making inferior hands fold when you would rather they call, but you can't always know in advance whether that will happen.

Raising to bluff is an unusual tactic in the lower limit games, and you won't see it done very often. Raising to semi-bluff, however, is very common, especially on the flop, and you'll use this tactic very frequently in your games.

Let's look at some examples of how to use each of these tactics in a real game.

Raising to Eliminate Players
Before the Flop
If you have AA or KK, you have the best chance of winning the hand if you play it against fewer players. It's unusual to make a straight or a flush with any pocket pair, because you'd be using only one of your cards to make the hand. Most of the times you win with a big pocket pair will be instances when you made two pair or did not improve your hand at all. In those cases, you'd rather be facing just two players than everybody at the table. A raise before the flop will help ensure that you're facing fewer players at the river.

If you have AK, you have an even more vulnerable hand than you do with pocket aces or kings. Although a preflop raise will usually reduce the field, there's another factor to consider: with Big Slick you're going to miss the flop most of the time anyway. Generally, I think it's best if you do not raise before the flop with

Big Slick. There are three instances, however, in which it's okay to do so:

1. *If you're in late position and no one else has called.* Your raise will knock out players behind you, so you'll have to play this hand against only a few players, which gives you a better chance to win it.

2. *If you think you can steal the blinds.* If you raise and happen to get called, perhaps by the big blind, you still figure to have the best hand before the flop most of the time.

3. *If another player has raised, and a reraise from you will force a player between you to call two or more bets cold.* Your reraise will usually force the player between you to fold, which increases the chances that you'll win the hand. If that player calls two bets cold, you'll have accomplished one of the other reasons for raising–to gain information.

On the Flop
There are two types of flops that you should routinely raise with when you hold AK:

1. *When you flop another ace or king.*

2. *When you flop 10JQ, to make an ace-high straight.*

Let's look at some specific examples:

You hold A♠ K♦. The flop is A♦ 9♥ 5♣.

If there's a bet ahead of you, you should raise to eliminate players who might draw out on you. Anyone holding four cards to a straight or a pocket pair is an underdog to your hand, and you don't want him to draw cheaply or for free.

You hold A♠ K♦. The flop is K♣ J♥ 8♥.

You just flopped top pair with top kicker. You'll normally have the best hand at this point, and you'll win it most of the time. You have to protect this hand, though. You do that by raising. Always raise when you flop top pair with top kicker. Just calling lets the other players in to try to beat you for the minimum bet.

You hold A♠ K♦. The flop is Q♣ J♥ 10♦.

You just flopped the nut straight. This type of flop poses a great danger for your hand because it's all high cards. Look at all of these hands that could possibly be out against you: QQ, JJ, 1010, QJ, Q10, and J10. These are all very reasonable hands that your opponents could be playing.

In addition, anyone whose hole cards are suited could see the flop, trying to pick up a four-flush to beat you on the river. Anyone holding an ace or a king could eventually hit his gutshot draw and cause you to split the pot. You have to raise to give all of these hands the worst possible odds to draw out on you.

You hold A♠ K♦. The flop is A♥ K♣ 8♣.
You have top two pair, but anyone holding a QJ, Q10, or J10 has a gutshot straight draw, and anyone with two clubs has a flush draw. Raise and make them pay to beat you.

AK isn't the only hand you must have to consider raising to eliminate players after the flop. Let's look at a few others:

You hold Q♣ 10♥. The flop is 10♣ 8♠ 4♥.
Raise. You do not want anyone holding AK, AQ, AJ, KQ, QJ, or a pocket pair below 10s to call. Your biggest fear is an overcard to the 10. An ace or a king will beat your pair of 10s, and a jack could complete the straight draw. Anyone holding 99, 77, 66, and 55 will often call to see the turn card if the pot is big enough and the price is right. If you flop top pair with a good kicker and you just call, you are inviting disaster.

You hold A♥ 9♣. The flop is 9♠ 5♣ 2♥.
Again, you have top pair with top kicker and probably have the best hand. The problem is that there are so many gaps between the ace and the 9. Look at how many hands can beat you if you get a card in the gap on the turn: AK, AQ, AJ, A10, KQ, KJ, K10, K9, QJ, Q10, Q9, J10, J9. You also have to worry about the backdoor flush draw and the two wheel cards on the flop. An ace, 3, 4, or 6 could complete the baby straight draw. Your hand is so vulnerable that it's easier to count the cards that help you rather than the cards

that hurt you. This is a hand you need to protect, so raise now to scare away other players.

You hold 5♥ 5♣. The flop is K♣ 9♠ 5♦.

Never slowplay a bottom set, especially if you can raise and knock someone out. A player holding a higher pocket pair, KJ, K10, QJ, Q10, J10, or a three-flush could easily beat you on the turn or river. You have the best hand. Make them pay to beat you.

You hold 9♥ 8♥. The flop is 10♣ 7♥ 6♦.

You flopped the nut straight, but there are still so many cards that can beat you. A 6, 7, 8, 9, 10, or jack could make someone else a higher straight or a full house. You have to eliminate players so your hand will stand up at the end.

I'm including this example because it recently happened to me. I held the 7♠ 6♠ when this exact flop hit the board. The player who held the 9♥ 8♥ in front of me had just called, thinking he would wait for the turn, when the bets double, to raise. The turn card was the 7♦, making me a full house and winning the hand for me. If the other player had raised on the flop, when he had the best hand, I would not have had the correct odds to call, so I would gladly have folded bottom two pair.

You hold 9♦ 2♦. The flop is 3♦ 5♦ 10♦.

You just completed a flush (but if you saw the flop with this hand, I hope you're in the big blind). The problem, though, is that your flush is only 9-high.

Anyone with a higher diamond will beat you if another comes on the turn or river. Your hand is good
at the moment but very vulnerable. Using the table
from Chapter 7, you can see that anyone holding a
higher diamond has only a 27.8% chance of getting
the flush to beat you.

Since you know you are going to win this hand almost
three out of four times, you should raise to give him
the worst possible odds to draw to the hand (and a
chance to fold). Sometimes your opponent will be
holding something like J♦ 8♣ and fold, not wanting
to risk being beat himself when another diamond
comes. On your good days, a player holding a higher
diamond will fold when you raise, another diamond
will come on the turn or river, and you will look soooo
good when you drag the pot. Congratulations on being
smart enough to know how to play the hand.

You hold 2♥ 2♣. The flop is A♠ A♣ 2♠.
Just like you can't afford to slowplay bottom set, you
can't afford to slowplay bottom full house. Do not
be lulled into a false sense of security just because you
have a full house and it is high on the scale of poker
hands. Anyone holding a pocket pair could hit it on the
turn or river to make a higher full house, and anyone
holding an ace and a 3 or above could hit his kicker
to make a higher full house also. There's also the very
real possibility of the dealer's running off a pair on
the turn and river. Sure, you're still a favorite against
these draws happening, but still, you'd rather they fold

and let you win the pot right there. It's better to win a small pot than to lose a big one, and that's what a raise to eliminate players will help you do.

Your poker hand in hold'em is always relative, because its strength depends largely on what cards are on the board. For example, what if I told you that you'd make four of a kind on your next hand? You'd be pretty excited. But what if I added that the board would be A♠ A♣ A♥ A♦ 2♣, and you'd hold 3♠ 3♥ against three other players? How do you feel about your four of a kind now?

Raising to Get a Free Card

Actually, it's not really a free card. It's a cheap card, usually costing one-half of a big bet (one full small bet) instead of the full big bet. Here's how it works in a nutshell: If you call $3 on the flop and $6 on the turn, you will, of course, have $9 invested on those two calls. If, however, you raise and make it $6 to call on the flop, your opponents will often check to you on the turn. It may be because they don't want to be raised again, it may be because you've convinced them that you have the better hand, or it may be because they truly don't know what else to do.

Whatever your opponents' reasons for checking may be, you can also check behind them, thereby not investing any money on the turn card. You've now paid only $6 on the flop and nothing on the turn, for a total of $6.

You see that by raising on the flop, you've saved $3 you would have spent if you'd just called on the flop and on the turn. You should learn to execute this valuable tactic well, because this situation arises often in hold'em games. If this tactic works for you only twice in an hour, you'll have saved one big bet per hour, which is quite a lot. Professional poker players feel that they are doing quite well if they can win just one to two big bets per hour, so you can see how learning a tactic worth one big bet per hour is so valuable.

Raising to get a free card works best on the flop, because the bet doubles on the next card. If you've raised before the flop, however, the other players will sometimes all check to you on the flop. You can then also check, and you all get to see the turn card for free. This happens less often but it's worth keeping in mind.

When you raise on the flop hoping to get a free card, it will usually be because you have one of two types of hands:

1. *A pair that's weak under these particular circumstances.* It could be top pair with a weak kicker or bottom pair with a good kicker (why not bottom pair with a weak kicker? Because you don't continue with hands that bad)! You could have a pocket pair that is beat by the board, but you don't think it paired any of your opponents' cards.

2. A straight- or flush- draw.

Let's look at some examples of these types of hands:

You're in the blind with K♥ 5♣. The flop comes K♠ 9♣ 3♥. There's a bet and you raise.

The other player will often check to you on the turn. If you like the turn card, or it improves your hand, or you feel that your pair of kings is the best hand, regardless of kicker, then you can bet it again. If the turn card doesn't help you, and your opponent checks into you, you can check and save a big bet. If it then turns out that your opponent had you beat with, say K♦ 8♦, then you got a free card when you had the worst hand. Drawing for free with the worst hand! It doesn't get any better than that, and it happened because you raised to get a free card.

You have A♦ 3♦. The flop is J♥ 6♣ 3♠. There's a bet and you raise.

If the bettor checks to you on the turn you can also check and see the river card before you have to put any more money in the hand. If you spike another ace or 3, you'll have gotten in an extra bet with a winning hand, which is the essence of all forms of poker. If you miss on the turn and the river, you will at least have gotten to see the river for free.

If you repeat this situation over and over during the course of a game, occasionally you'll hit your hand, and you'll win much more than the cost of that little $3 raise on the flop. There's also the possibility that your small pair is the best hand at the showdown, and you'll win the pot because you didn't have to throw it away when someone bet into you. Your raise on the flop kept that from happening.

You have K♠ 10♠ and the flop is A♣ J♥ 8♦.
You have a straight draw, but it's a gutshot, and you'd clearly like to play this hand as cheaply as possible. If it's bet into you, raise. If the bettor then checks on the turn, you can also check if you missed.

You have A♣ J♣. The flop is K♥ 9♣ 3♣.
You don't have anything yet, but you have the potential to make a big hand. Raise on the flop. The player who bet into you won't know if you have the king with a good kicker or if you're on a straight- or flush-draw. If you make the flush on the turn, then you can bet with a winning hand, knowing that the pot is a little bit bigger because you raised on the flop. If you miss on the turn and the others check to you, then you can also check and continue to draw for free.

Raising to Gain Information
Sometimes many of your opponents will have folded anyway, and you won't need to raise to force them out of the hand. Maybe you'll find yourself left with just one or two opponents, and you'll want to have a good idea of what they might be holding. So you'll raise anyway. That's called raising to gain information, and it works best before the flop and on the flop.

RAISING

Before the Flop

Before the flop, the most you can know about a player's hand are the basic odds of his being dealt any two-card combination. You also know what position he's in relative to the blinds, what the pot odds were when he called to see the flop, whether he called a raise and whether he, himself, was a raiser.

If you know something about reading tells, then you might have an idea how he feels about his hand. Does he seem to be satisfied with the way things went before the flop? If so, then he has a good starting hand. Is he uneasy or unhappy about a preflop raise? If so, then his cards may not be that good for his position.

Suppose he raises from middle position before the flop, and it's just the two of you in the hand. So far, you don't know a whole lot about his hand. He could have any pocket pair or any two big cards. If you just call, you'll never know any more than that. If you want more information about his hand, all you have to do is ask him for it. You have to realize that the way to do that is to reraise. Do it now while the bets are still small and you have less money invested in the hand. How he reacts to that reraise from you will help you narrow down his possible holdings.

If he just calls, he's told you a lot. Mainly, he's said that he can't tell if the hand he has is clearly superior to yours without seeing the flop. He wants to see the flop before investing any more money. If he reraises you, then he's telling you the opposite. Pocket aces and kings are two hands with which no one should mind reraising a sole opponent before the flop.

If he reraises, then you can put him on pocket aces or kings. If you know your opponent is a little looser than most, you might want to give him credit for pocket queens or jacks or possibly AK suited.

On the Flop
Raising to gain information on the flop is a very common tactic. Basically, you want to know the answer to one of two questions:

1. *At the moment, does my opponent have a better hand than I do?*

2. *Is he on a draw?*

Let's look at an example of this sort of situation:

You have A♣ 8♣. Your opponent raised before the flop, and the flop is A♠ 9♥ 5♦. He bets into you, telling you that he has at least a pair of aces.
Whether your opponent actually does have the aces is something you don't yet know. If you just call here, and then call again on the turn and the river, you'll never know where you stand. He could have kings and be giving you a chance to fold. Here, you raise to gain information. If he folds, then it was your raise that told him that you have an ace or better, and he couldn't beat that. If he reraises you, then you've found

out what you wanted to know. Consider the following hands (again, "s" means "suited"):

AA, KK, QQ, JJ, 1010, 99, AKs, AQs, AJs, AK, AQ, AJ, KQs, KJs, K10s, KQ, KJ, K10, QJ, Q10, J10s

There are 160 different hands represented here! These are all hands that he could have raised with before the flop. When he bet into you on the flop, he could have had any one of these hands. If you know this player, maybe you know that if he flopped nothing in this spot he would have checked it. Go through the above list and eliminate any hand that would have been nothing on the flop.

Now, go through the list and eliminate any hand that would have been something on the flop, but you think most players would have checked. Since he didn't check on the flop, he doesn't have those hands.

The next step is to eliminate hands with which he would just have called your raise. He didn't just call, so he doesn't have those hands. Now look at the remaining hands. Which of these hands seems to fit with what you know about how he played his hand so far?

In most situations, I think AA, 99, AKs and AK are excellent candidates. I think he positively has one of these hands, even though I'm not sure exactly which one it is. I don't have to know which hand he has, all I have to know is that he's got me beat and I don't have the right odds to continue with the hand.

I'm going to fold, but there's one more mental exercise I'm going to perform before I throw the hand away. I ask myself the Big Picture Question: "Is there any way he could have played his hand this way with a hand worse than mine?" Maybe my answer is "No." In that case, I'm certainly right to fold now.

Using one type of reasoning, I've determined that his hand is much better than mine. Using another type of reasoning, I've also determined that his hand can't possibly be worse than mine. Putting the two together, it's a cinch I'm beat.

I want you to go back and look at what could be called the tempo, or cadence, of the hand you just analyzed. Before the flop it was bet-raise-call. After the flop is was bet-raise-reraise and then (after analyzing the hand) fold. I want you to know that ninety-nine times out of a hundred, the after-the-flop action would have been bet-raise-reraise-call. Instead it was bet-raise-reraise-fold.

Have you ever seen anyone raise and then fold when it was reraised, when he had to call only one more small bet to see the next card? Who folds after he has raised and has to call only one bet to see the next card? You do, that's who! If you're beat, and you know it, then there's absolutely no reason you should call another bet this hand. Too many players will call that last reraise because it happens so quickly and they don't give it too much thought.

RAISING

Don't fall into the trap of making automatic plays just because you're in the middle of a heated contest. Your raise served its purpose–you found out what you wanted to know about your opponent's hand. It's only one hand, so let it go. Take comfort in the fact that you're saving a bet where you know other players would be losing that bet and subsequent ones.

Raising to Get Value from Your Hand

Of the five reasons to raise, this one is the easiest to understand. Whenever you have the best hand and you want to make the other players pay the price for having second-best hands, all you have to do is raise. Let's look at an example:

You have A♦ 9♦ and the board is K♦ 9♥ 5♦ 10♦ with the river card to come.
If there's a bet, you should raise. Why? Well, let's see:

You're not trying to eliminate any players. In fact, you want everyone to call this bet and raise.

You're not trying to get a free card on the river. In fact, it costs just as much to raise on the turn as it does to bet on the river.

You're not trying to gain information. You don't really care what anyone else has; you're a big favorite over whatever it is. Anyone with a set needs the board to pair, and they have only ten outs. Anyone holding

J♦ Q♦ needs the A♦ or the 9♦ to make a straight flush, and you're the only one who knows those cards aren't in the deck because they're in your hand. Anyone holding two pair has only eight outs to make a full house.

You're certainly not bluffing. Bluffing would be betting without so much as a pair. You've got the nut flush.

So why are you raising?

You are raising to get other players to put more money into a pot you expect to win. That's betting for value. You don't always have to have the nuts to be able to bet for value. If you think you have the best hand at the table, you can also raise for value, even if your hand isn't the best hand possible. The key is knowing when your hand is probably the best, even if it's not the best possible hand. Let's look at another example:

You're in the big blind with 6♥ 5♥. The player on your left raises, making it two bets to go. Two other players call. With 7 to 1 odds, you call too. The flop is 8♣ 5♠ 2♥. You check, the preflop raiser bets, and the other two players fold. You call because you can beat A♣ K♦, you're getting 9 to 1 pot odds, and you're against only one other player, who might check when the turn card comes. The turn card is the 6♣.
You now have two pair. What can you determine now about your chances? If you know your opponent would raise in early position only with big pairs or big cards,

then you know you have him beat with only one card to come, so you should raise.

The phrase "only one card to come" is a very important one in the game of Texas hold'em. Why? Because that phrase sums up a particular situation while implying a relatively safe prediction about the future. There are sports with similar phrases.

What if I told you that Jeff Gordon was the leader during the Indianapolis 500? Not much information there. What if I now specified that Jeff Gordon was the leader–with one lap to go? See the difference?

What if you knew that Nick Faldo was leading the US Open by two strokes? Again, not very exciting, because two strokes is not that big a lead among professionals. What if I added that Nick Faldo was leading the US Open by two strokes–with one hole to go? It means something entirely different now, doesn't it?

In the last example we looked at, if your opponent has A♣ A♠ or K♥ K♦, then he has only eight outs with which to beat you on the river: the two other aces or kings, three 8s or three 2s. You are a 5 to 1 favorite not to lose this hand with only one card to come. You can raise for value with confidence, even though you know you don't have the best possible hand. You have the best probable hand, and that's good enough.

Raising to Bluff or to Semi-Bluff
To Bluff

Bluffing is a big part of the game, so big in fact that there's an entire chapter on the subject later in this book. Betting to bluff, however, is not the same thing as raising to bluff. Raising to bluff, especially when all the cards are out, is a tactic that is very seldom used except at the highest limit games ($40/$80 and above).

In those hands, decisions about calling and folding are based on reading a player's actions in a specific hand. Plus, you're getting great pot odds to call that last raise. Usually, the pot is so big that it is mathematically correct to make a "crying call" rather than lose the entire pot for want of calling one last bet.

I saw raising as a bluff used in a lower limit game only once in the last year. I'll share that example with you:

Player A raised before the flop. Only Player B called. The flop was 9♣ 6♥ 3♦. Player A checked. Player B checked right behind him. The turn was the A♠. Player A bet and Player B raised him. Player A folded immediately. Player B showed K♥ Q♥ and said, "If you had an ace, you would have bet it on the flop." There are three reasons this raise as a bluff worked:

1. Player B knew his opponent. A player who raises before the flop will usually have AA, KK, QQ, or at least AK or AQ. He will almost always bet on the flop

against a single opponent, especially with a ragged flop. Since Player A didn't bet, Player B deduced that he didn't have one of these hands.

2. Player B, even though he may have believed that he had the best hand after the flop, did not bet. Why? Because there were five small bets in the pot, and if Player B bet after Player A checked, Player A would be getting pot odds of 6 to 1 to call. There are a lot of hands with which you can call when you have only a 1 out of 7 chance of winning and the pot gives you the correct odds to call.

3. Player B, by not betting on the flop, kept the pot small and ensured that it offered the worst possible odds. The rake and the jackpot drop had reduced the pot to only four small bets (or only two big bets), by the time the turn card came. When Player A got raised on the turn, he realized that he did not have the right odds to call a raise with the prospect of having to call another bet on the river. He was getting odds of 7 to 1 to call the first raise. Even if his hand was as good as a pocket pair, he was 22 to 1 to hit it on the river.

To Semi-Bluff

Semi-bluffing is defined as betting with a hand that, if called, probably isn't the best hand at the moment, but has a chance to improve with more cards to come. It's a cross between betting as a bluff and betting for value, when you know there's not much value at the moment.

Consider the following example:

You have A♦ 3♥. The flop is K♣ 8♠ 3♦, and a player before you bets.
You might now raise as a semi-bluff. This play is a good one because three different factors are working for you all at the same time:

1. You might actually have the best hand at this point, and everyone will fold. Another player could be holding another 8 with a bad kicker. He might fold, not knowing he has you beat.

2. Your raise could induce the other players to check to you on the next round, thereby giving you a free card and an opportunity to check again. You now get to see both the turn and the river cards for free, if all goes well.

3. You can improve your hand. If you hit an ace or another 3, you will probably win the hand.

A fairly advanced tactic paid off for you in this instance, and you can see why it's useful. If you're going to try raising as a semi-bluff on the flop, there are four important things you should know:

1. Your real goal is to win the pot right then. If there's any chance that you will get a caller or two, however reluctant they are, you should generally not raise to semi-bluff. The exception to that rule is if you know your raise on the flop will induce your opponent to

check to you on the next round, even when he has a very good hand.

Semi-bluff opportunities arise very frequently during the course of a hold'em game. It's very important that you understand and truly believe that your real goal in semi-bluffing is to win the pot right then. If you misplay your hand in these situations, you'll have a big leak in your game, because situations like this arise so frequently. I'm therefore going to restate the above rule to make it very clear how to play:

If you're in a semi-bluff situation and you feel that your raise will not win the pot for you right then, you should usually fold rather than raise (or call).

2. Semi-bluffing does not work well when you are facing a lot of players, regardless of what the flop is. If there are a lot of players to see the flop, someone will usually think he has the right odds to see the next card, whether there was a raise on the flop or not. Semi-bluffing also doesn't work against players who habitually play every hand and call every bet.

3. Semi-bluffing does not work well when the flop is of obvious help to anyone who should be holding high cards, like players in early position or players who raised before the flop. In other words, if you can tell by a player's position and the cards on the flop that he'll be calling any bets, you should not bet as a semi-bluff.

4. You shouldn't semi-bluff in last position if you fear the possibility of a check-raise. Putting in two bets on the flop defeats the purpose of semi-bluffing. Worse, a bet from another player lets you know that you certainly don't have the best hand, and any draw you have may not win if you do hit it. If another player has flopped a set or top two pair and is betting for value, you'll win this hand only about 2.5% of the time if you play to the river, and about 1% otherwise.

In the example above, where you hold A♦ 3♥ and the flop is K♣ 8♠ 3♦, you have a good semi-bluff opportunity. If, however, the flop were K♣ J♠ 3♦ or K♣ 8♠ 3♣ with a lot of players, you couldn't semi-bluff. In those cases, if someone bets, you should fold. In the first flop, it's just too likely that someone has a straight draw, if not a pair of kings or even kings and jacks, and will certainly call. In the second flop, the two clubs on the board with a lot of players still in will certainly get you some callers if you bet.

Summary

When you go back and look at the five reasons to raise, you can see that they are interconnected. In other words, it's nearly impossible to raise chiefly for one reason without making it seem that you could be raising for another reason. If you raise to eliminate players, you might also get a free card, gain information, get value from your hand, and possibly make your opponent think that you are semi-bluffing.

RAISING

If you raise to get a free card, you're probably also getting value from your hand, and you might eliminate someone. If you raise to gain information, you might also eliminate someone, get a free card, and get value from your hand. If you raise to semi-bluff, you might force someone to fold, get a free card, or get some information.

Raising at the right time—and knowing why you're raising—is one of the hallmarks of a great player. It's very important that you understand everything in this chapter. Using the tactic of raising correctly, along with correctly selecting your before-the-flop hand, will help you become the second-best type of hold'em player there is: Tight/Aggressive (other types of hold'em players include Tight/Passive, Loose/Aggressive and Loose/Passive).

Tight/Aggressive means that you see the flop with relatively few hands. When you do decide to play a hand, you take charge of the hand and play aggressively. The best way to be aggressive is to be a raiser, and now you know five good reasons to raise.

Test Your Knowledge #4

If Tight/Aggressive is only the second-best type of player, what do you think the best type of poker player is?
Answer at the end of the chapter.

Freerolling

Freerolling is simply being in the enviable position of having the nuts with a draw to an even better hand. The most common freerolling situation is when you have the nut flush draw but first make a straight with more cards to come.

For example, you might have A♥ Q♥ when the board is K♦ J♥ 4♥ 10♠. You have the nut straight, and you'd have to split the pot with anyone else holding AQ. Any heart on the river, however, will give you the nut flush, and the other player with AQ would get none of the pot instead of half of it.

This example illustrates the benefit of being suited: it gives you an additional out. For example, if you have 10♣ 9♣ and the flop is J♣ 8♠ 7♦, you have the nut straight. If the turn card is another club, then you have a draw to a backdoor flush, which will beat anyone else also holding a 109, or anyone who made a straight on the turn.

How do you play your hand when you are freerolling? There are three things you must always do: raise, raise and raise. It doesn't matter if you don't make the draw; you still have the nuts. You'll get in extra bets with a winning hand, and that's the essence of winning poker. There is one situation that you should watch out for: when you're freerolling and it's four bets to go on the turn. With that many bets, if your freeroll draw isn't to the nuts, one of the other raisers probably has it.

RAISING

Structure Your Learning

Assignment #8

The next time you play in your regular game, I want you to keep track of every time you raise. Take a notebook with you with enough space for a separate entry for each reason to raise. For the sake of brevity, you can write EP for eliminate players, FC for free card, GI for gain information, GV for get value from your hand and SB for semi-bluff, all on separate pages.

Whenever you raise, decide what the main reason for your raise is, and record the result on the appropriate page. All you want to know is if the purpose of your raise was successful. For example, if the primary purpose of your raise was to get a free card, and your opponent bet into you on the next round anyway, you would record a "No" or some other negative remark on your "FC" page. Perhaps a "+" or a "-" would work for you. "FCN" (no) or "FCY" (yes) would also tell you what you want to know.

Compile this list until you have at least thirty entries in each of four different categories (preferably in all five). It'll probably take more than one or two games to get that many entries on your list. Whenever you're collecting statistical data like these, the general rule of thumb is: the more the better. If you choose to collect more than thirty samples in each category for this exercise, you'll have even more reliable results when you analyze the data.

Once you've completed your data collection and you have at least the minimum number of entries, compute the percentage of "yes," or positive marks, you have in each category. Next, arrange the categories by percentage score, with the lowest score at the top and the highest score at the bottom of your list.

If you're going to work on improving your game, this exercise will tell you where you have the best time and effort to result ratio. The reason for raising that's working the least for you (the one at the top of your list) is the area in which you have the most room to improve with the least effort.

After you've done this exercise and you've worked on this aspect of your game for a while, put it away temporarily and don't worry about it. If you've done the exercise and the work, the subject of raising will be on your mind anyway. After you've read the rest of this book and another six months to a year have passed, do this exercise again. I think you'll be very pleased with your results.

Answer to Test Your Knowledge Question #4

The best type of poker player is what I would call "The Chameleon." A Chameleon is a player whose superior understanding of the game allows him to assume the identity and playing style of any one of the four types of players when he decides it's in his best interests. The best way to become a Chameleon is to start out by being a Tight/Aggressive player.

PLAYING IN THE BLINDS

If you're in the big blind and no one raises before the flop, then how to play in the big blind is one of the easiest decisions you'll ever have to make in this game. Unless you have pocket aces or kings, all you have to do is check, see the flop, and decide how to play from there. It's seldom that easy, though. There's often a preflop raise, which gives you an opportunity to make a costly mistake if you don't play the hand correctly.

Most beginning players play incorrectly in this area. They play too loose when they're raised in the blinds, especially in the big blind. Their thinking usually goes something like this: "Well, I'm already in for one bet, I might as well call one more bet to see the flop." This view is the wrong one to take in this situation for four reasons:

1. In a way, the money that you already have in the pot did not come from you. Once money is put into the pot, for the purposes of making decisions, it doesn't matter where it came from. It's as if it came from nowhere. One of the statements that you'll often hear from poker players is, "I've already invested X dollars in this hand, so I have to call again." This is very erroneous thinking.

2. If you are in a $3/$6 hold'em game, then the blinds are $3 and $1, if you don't call the other $2 in the small blind. This is a total of $4 per round. In a ten-handed game, this comes to 40¢ per hand. Even if you must think of the money you've already invested–which, as I said, is the wrong way to play–you should think of it as only 40¢ and not as the $3 you have in the big blind.

3. In taking the "money-I've-invested" perspective, you've missed the correct way to see the situation, which is mainly from a pot odds point of view. When you're facing a raise when in one of the blinds, your decision whether to call should be based on how much it costs you to call versus how much money is in the pot, or how much you think will be in the pot after everyone else calls. It should not be based on how much you've already invested.

4. You must also take into account what you think the preflop raiser has. If you think he has a premium hand, you have to know what the odds are that your hand can beat his. You then have to compare those odds to the odds being offered by the pot when making your decisions to call or fold.

Preflop Calling Odds

If you're in the big blind and you hear the word, "Raise," you should automatically begin a decision-making process while the action is coming back around to you. Here's what you might be thinking:

"All right, I'm in the big blind. The player on my left called, the next player folded, and there are two bets in the pot. The next player raised, making a total of four bets in the pot. Everyone else folded around to me, and I either have to call one more bet or fold.

"The pot is offering me 4 to 1 odds, and the player between me and the raiser will probably just call also, so my implied odds are likely to be 5 to 1. Therefore, I need a 1 out of 6 chance of winning this hand just to break even in the long run. Do the cards I'm holding right now give me that 1 out of 6 chance of winning, assuming the raiser has what he's supposed to have?"

Maybe your situation was a little different:

"I'm in the big blind and there's been a raise. Everyone else has folded around to me. There are three bets in the pot, and the raiser obviously has a good hand. Do I have at least a 1 out of 4 chance of winning this hand?"

Or maybe what happened was:

"I'm in the big blind. There's been a raise. Everyone has called, and now it's my turn to act. There are nineteen

bets in the pot, and I can call without fear of another raise, because the raiser is on my immediate left. Do I have a 1 out of 20 chance of winning this hand?"

To keep things simple, both of these examples ignore the effect of the rake and the jackpot drop, if there is one. If the rake is $4 maximum per hand, and the jackpot drop is $1 per hand, that's quite a lot when the pot is very small. Your odds could be reduced from 3 to 1 to 1.5 to 1 when there's just you and the raiser in the hand.

On the other hand, the larger the pot, the less effect the rake has on your pot odds. Remember to take the rake and the jackpot drop into account when figuring your pot odds and making your decision.

If you're in the small blind, you have a different situation. Instead of the full $3, you have to call only $2 more, so the math is a little different. When the action is coming around to you, you have to keep track of the size of the pot in terms of actual dollars, not just number of bets.

If there are six callers including the big blind, then there's $19 in the pot. You have to divide your $2 call into $19 to get your odds. In this case it's 9.5 to 1, whereas if you had to call the whole bet, your odds would be only 6.33 to 1.

PLAYING IN THE BLINDS

What hands should you call a raise with, if you're in the big blind? As I've said, people generally play too loose in this situation, often because of two factors:

1. You rarely know just what the raiser has. My years of experience have taught me that if you're a typical player, you'll underestimate or just plain ignore the strength of the raiser's hand, and you'll overestimate the value of your own hand. These two mistakes conspire to encourage you to call and see the flop with a lot of hands that should be folded.

2. You can never be sure of how the future action in the hand will go. It may require you to call bets and raises that you'd rather not.

Refer to the list of groups of hands in Chapter 9, the chapter called "Starting Hands." In the big blind, you would certainly want to call a preflop raise with these hands. These are all good, profitable hands, if you have the right pot odds to see the flop. Other hands do not play well head-up, especially if the other player has raised, telling you that he probably has a Group 1 or 2 hand. Low hands can and do win, but you can go a long time between wins with them, so you need big odds to play these inferior hands.

If you're in the small blind, you should play even fewer hands than you do in the big blind. Can you see why? It's because when you're in the small blind, there's another player behind you who can reraise, thereby giving you worse odds and making it more unlikely for you to win the hand (I'm talking about the big blind, in case you didn't realize it). When you're in the small blind, remember that you'll be in the worst possible position throughout the hand. You can't win the hand by checking, and bluffs from an early position are harder to pull off.

There's one more thing to consider when deciding to call a preflop raise from either blind. You have terrible position for the entire hand, and the raiser is in a much better spot. Before you call, therefore, you need to know how well the raiser plays. If he's a genuinely good player, you should not call as often with average hands. If he's a bad player, or happens to be playing very loosely, you can also play a little more loosely.

Remember, your profit in this game comes from the mistakes your opponents make. If the preflop raiser is a player who doesn't make many mistakes, and his raise tells you that he wants to win this hand, maybe you should think about letting him win it. You can win the next one.

Structure Your Learning
Assignment #9
The next time you play in your regular game, keep track of every time the pot is raised before the flop. Watch the big blind and record the result of how he plays. Count only those hands where the big blind stays in the whole time and turns his hand face up at the end of the hand. Do not include hands in which

the big blind does not play to the river or call a bet on the river.

All you need to keep track of is whether the big blind wins the hand. Keep two separate records: one for those times when other players call a preflop raise in the big blind, and one for those times when you're the one in the big blind.

Practice this exercise for two consecutive playing sessions. Compare your winning percentages to those of the other players. For the next two playing sessions, after that, just keep track of how you fare when calling raises before the flop in the big blind.

Your winning percentage should improve as you keep correct big blind play in mind. Record your results and keep them where you can easily find them later. After you've completed this book and a year or so has passed, try checking yourself again and comparing those results to the first time you tried this strategy. Good luck!

PLAYING IN LATE POSITION

For purposes of this discussion, late position is defined as being on the button or one or two seats to the right of the button. Don't forget the one major inherent advantage of being in late position: you have more information than your opponents had when deciding what to bet on each round. You're in a good position throughout the hand, so you also have a lesser chance of being raised when you call a bet.

Before the Flop

When you are in late position and the action comes around to you, other players may or may not have already called the big blind. Whether you're first in the pot or not, there's one thing that you must do every time you make a decision regarding whether to play your hand: *look at the players between you and the big blind and determine their player profiles.*

I'm not saying you have to know everything about your opponents. You're mainly interested in knowing if they are the type of players that will defend their blinds if you raise. Are they passive or aggressive? Are they tight or loose? Does the player on the button *always* play his button? Some low limit players see the flop with *any* two cards when they are on the button.

When you're in late position, no one else has entered the pot, and you have what would ordinarily be a calling hand, you should strongly consider raising, especially if you have an ace in your hand. There are many good reasons for this play:

1. If you are one or two seats to the right of the button, this raise might force the player(s) between you and the button to fold, thereby making you the last player (by position) to have a hand. This is called **buying the button.**

2. You might force everyone to fold and you'll win the blinds. Don't make the common beginner's mistake of thinking that it's not worth winning a very small pot made up of only the blinds. It's a very valuable win for you, because that small pot will give you the chips you need to post the blinds yourself and play another round.

3. A play that wins you the blinds, when successful, adds significantly to your hourly rate, which is what all of this is really about. If you can successfully steal the blinds only twice an hour, you will be winning almost three small bets per hour, which is almost 1.5 big bets per hour. Remember how I said that the average professional hold'em player considers himself successful if he can earn 1-2 big bets per hour? I know a few players whose overall skill at the game I would consider to be mediocre-to-average, but they're professional late position players and blind stealers. There's no reason you can't be, too.

4. When you raise in late position, your opponents won't know for sure which one of the five reasons to raise it is that you have in mind, although they will often correctly suspect that it's primarily a move based on position and very small pot odds. In other words, they will believe that most of the time you raise in late position, you're raising mainly to eliminate players. They won't be certain, though, and it's always good to keep your opponents guessing.

5. By making this type of play regularly (don't overdo it, or your opponents will just start calling you all the time), you're setting your opponents up for a future play. You won't always have a second-rate hand when you raise in late position. Sometimes you'll have that AA, KK or AKs when you raise, and you'll make a lot of money from the players who call you all the way down, just because they think you have K9 or Q10, which they can beat.

6. If you buy the button and one (or both) of the blinds calls your preflop raise, you'll have position on him (them) throughout the hand.

7. If you have an ace, and you raise in late position as the first one in, you may find yourself against just one opponent on the river. In that case, your ace is a *big* card. You might win with just ace-high against that one player, where king-high and queen-high won't win. With an ace, your raise was a fairly safe play.

You have an entirely different situation if you're in late position and a lot of players have entered the pot ahead of you. Now you have to consider a few things:

1. The players in early position probably have very good cards.

2. The players in middle position have good drawing hands, otherwise one of them would have raised before the flop.

3. Because of their position and the pot odds they were getting when they called, other players (besides you) in late position might have longshot draws, such as small pairs and medium suited connectors (7♠ 6♠, 6♥ 5♥, or even 5♣ 4♣).

4. One of the players in early position might have limped in with a Group 1 hand (AA, KK, QQ, JJ, AKs) and is waiting to reraise if you raise.

5. If such a reraise happens, one of the other players might want to make it three or four bets to go just for the sake of building the pot.

PLAYING IN LATE POSITION

The more players there are in the hand, the more possible variations there are in the way the hand will be played. Two players who have the four options of folding, calling, raising, and reraising could play a betting round one of sixteen different ways (4 x 4=16). Eight players who have those same options could theoretically play that same betting round one of 65,536 different ways! Of course, not every option is as equally likely as all of the other options. For example, I don't think you'll ever see everyone reraise and then fold!

In any event, if there are a lot of players in the pot to see the flop and you're in late position, your best strategy is to play defensively if you don't have a premium hand. You can do this in a few ways:

1. *Not raising with two big unsuited cards.* The only big hand you will normally make with these two cards is a straight, which is unlikely given that you haven't yet seen the flop. Besides, it's already too likely that you're beat before the flop. The most common outcome is that you'll pair one of your hole cards and your kicker will be useless.

2. *Raising only for just the right reasons, and folding after the flop if you miss.* If your cards are suited and connected, then you have two ways to win. If you feel that the game conditions are to your liking, you can consider raising from late position to get value from your hand. You have to be sensible about it, however. You have to be willing and able to make a superior,

professional-quality play when you see the flop: *throw the hand away on the flop if you miss or only get a small piece of it.* For example, if you have 6♠ 5♠ and the flop is A♣ J♥ 7♦, do not try to make the straight.

Being able to raise for the right reason before the flop and then throw the hand away on the flop is one of the characteristics of a great player. Do not become committed to defending the hand just because you raised before the flop, as you will see bad players do.

Remember, once money goes into the pot, it's as if that money came from nowhere. It's just there. It did not come from you. How much money you personally have put into playing a hand is not a factor to consider when making any subsequent decision regarding that hand.

You can also raise with small pocket pairs before the flop in late position, if you can also throw these hands away on the flop if you miss. If there are eight other players in the hand, you will be getting 15-1 odds on your preflop raise. You can afford to miss quite a few times on the flop and still make a big profit in the long run if you play these hands the right way.

3. *Not playing all hands just because you're in late position.* Too many players think it's okay to play every hand from a late position. There are a lot of great advantages to playing in late position, but the mere fact that you're in late position cannot turn purely garbage hands into premium hands. Do not play hands like

K♦ 6♥, 7♥ 2♣, 9♠ 4♠, Q♣ 5♥, J♦ 3♠ or 10♣ 4♥, just because you're in late position and you're getting big pot odds.

Here's a little secret: you can never get big enough pot odds to play garbage hands like these unless you're in the big blind and no one has raised. To slightly paraphrase that old saying: "You can't make chicken salad out of chicken crap."

After the Flop

Before the flop your hand could turn out to be anything in the end. One good thing about the flop is that when you see it, you will know exactly what your hand is and exactly what the odds of improving it by the river are. Play after the flop is fairly automatic in most instances, because you either have a hand or you don't, and you're either drawing to a straight or a flush or you're not.

If you have what you think is the best hand, you should play in a way that protects your lead. The flop is when most players will fold if they missed, and a bet or a raise from you will help them do so.

Don't give free cards on the flop if you have any kind of hand at all, and you think your opponents will fold if you bet. Betting and raising to eliminate players works best before the flop and on the flop.

If you showed strength before the flop by raising, then in the absence of any obvious signs that you could be beat, you should usually continue to give the impression that you have a strong hand. Give your opponents an opportunity to fold on the flop, especially if they've checked to you.

An opponent who checks and calls on both the flop and the turn could very likely be on a draw. Pay particular attention to the river card and be alert if it looks like it could have completed a draw for your opponent.

For example, if the board is K♥ J♣ 5♣ 8♠, and the river card is either the A♥ or 9♥, and he bets into you, he very likely is holding Q♦ 10♠ and has made his open end straight on the river. If the river card is another club, and he bets into you after having checked to you twice, then he has likely made a club flush.

If a third suited card comes on the river and a player who has been checking to you comes out betting, how do you know for sure that he has just made his flush? Well, you can never be 100% certain. He's representing a flush, but he may or may not have one.

What you have to do is look at the situation from his point of view. If he doesn't have a flush, then that flush card on the river looks just as scary to him as it does to you, yet he bet it anyway. Don't overlook the fact that even though that's a flush card on the river, it could have made him just a straight or a good two pair, and he's betting that it didn't make you a flush.

PLAYING IN LATE POSITION

When all of the cards are out and you're in last position, one of two things will happen. Either your opponent will check to you, or he'll bet into you. At this point you should think of all possible poker hands as falling into one of four categories:

1. *Low-strength hands.* These are hands that were possibly on a straight or a flush draw and missed. After the river card comes, this hand might be only ace- or king-high. It might also be a low pair that the player knows can't win a showdown.

2. *Medium-strength hands.* These are hands like top pair with a good kicker, two pair, and three of a kind if the board is paired.

3. *Very good hands.* These hands would be a set, a straight or a flush that is not the nuts, and maybe top two pair if no straight or flush is possible.

4. *The nuts.* Obviously, this is the best possible hand. Think about how likely it is that your opponent has made the nuts, especially if making it required hitting a gutshot straight draw or a backdoor flush.

When your opponent is first and he checks to you, he most likely has either a medium strength hand or the nuts. The reason that he'd check a medium strength hand to you is that with such a hand he has very little to gain by betting. Your hand could easily be a lot worse than his, and he won't win a bet from you when you fold. Your hand could also be far better than his, and he'll lose a bet (and the pot), when you call or raise. Your hand could also be close to his in strength. Not knowing how close, he'll just check.

Why would a player check, not just raise, to you if he had the nuts? The nuts is always a great candidate for a check-raise. If he's playing cards you wouldn't expect for his position, or if the turn and river cards gave him a good, unexpected hand, he will often consider a check-raise.

If your sole opponent bets into you, he probably has one of the other two types of hands: the low strength hand or the very good hand. Why would he bet a totally busted hand or only an ace-high into you? Well, he obviously cannot check and win. His bet is a bluff.

The reason that he'd bet a very good hand into you is that he's betting for value and wants to get paid off on the end. Why make a good hand if you're not going to make the other players pay for the privilege of making the second-best hands?

Structure Your Learning

Assignment #10

If you're in late position, you'd probably raise before the flop with the following hands ("s" is for "suited"):

AA	KK	QQ	JJ
AKs	AQs	AK	KQs

There are forty hands represented here. If you raise with only these hands, your opponents will always know that you're raising for value and to eliminate players. They don't have to worry about your raising primarily to take advantage of your late position. Your hand will always be easy to read. Add to your late position raise list the following hands:

1010	99	88	77
AJs	A10s	A9s	KJs

You've added another forty hands to your list. Now when you raise, it'll be equally likely that you're raising for value or raising to take advantage of your position. If your opponents catch on, and they eventually will, they'll know that when you raise in late position, it's 50-50 that your raise is for one reason or the other.

If you add another forty hands to your list, odds will be 2 to 1 against your having any of the first list hands when you raise. I recommend this ratio based on my years of experience at the table. This mix of hands will give you the best chance of confusing your opponents, making your hands harder to read and winning you the best possible profit in this situation in the long run.

Your assignment is to decide for yourself what you want those additional forty hands to be. Take the time and effort to write them down before you go to the game. Before you read this chapter, you'd already selected what hands to raise with before the flop in late position. Now you should have quite a few more hands on that list. Here's what I want you to do: in your notebook, keep track of how you do with the new hands the next few times you play in your usual game.

Record what percent of the time these new hands win the pot for you, and modify and adjust your list as you see fit. Every player plays in a different game, and what works well against one type of table lineup may not work as well at another table. Or it may work even better! Save these results in your notes for the game so you can make a comparison when you take another sample some time in the future.

15

STEALING THE BLINDS

The difference between raising to take advantage of your late position and raising to steal the blinds is mainly one of intent. Often you'll be in the same position, raising with the same cards, in the same situation. Only you will know if you're taking advantage of your late position (and want someone to call), or trying to steal the blinds (and want no one to call).

There are a few more tips to add to last chapter's list when your intent is to steal the blinds:

1. Do not limp in with Group 1 hands. Usually, one of the best ways to disguise the strength of your hand is just to call when a raise would normally be more appropriate. In this case, your raise works in just the opposite way. Since your opponents expect you to raise in late position anyway, you can disguise the strength of your hand by doing what looks natural for your position. Raise. They will rarely be sure that you're raising because you hold AA, KK, QQ or AKs.

2. When you take a seat in a hold'em game, closely observe the play of the three players to your left when they are in the big blind. If you happen to know these players and their profiles already, then so much the better. You're going to select a victim here, so you're scouting the turf in much the same way a burglar cases several houses at once to determine which one offers the best chance of his pulling off a successful robbery.

Watch these three players and then determine which one of the three is the least likely to defend (that is, call) when it is raised before the flop and he's in the big blind. Whichever one of the three players folds the most is your new victim. You should wait until this player is in the big blind to try your raise-steal move, because this will give you the best chance of success while you're still learning the game.

3. If your primary intent is to steal the blinds, you can raise with many more hands than you would if your intent were only to take advantage of your late position. Before you read further, can you see why? It's because if you performed the exercise described in the previous paragraph, you have a much higher chance of success than if you tried to steal at random.

You can now raise with pocket pairs of 5s and above, any time you have an ace or a king, regardless of your kicker, and when your hole cards are both 9 or higher.

If your intended victim in the big blind folds, then it doesn't matter what your cards were. If he calls, you're still in a good situation. His hand will be easy to read. Since he called in a spot where he almost never does, it must be very good. You have position on him throughout the hand, though. The combination of your having a read on his hand and position is enough to overcome any weakness in your hand after the flop. In the long run, you'll make a profit on this play.

4. If all three of the players on your left play very loosely, and they almost always defend their big blinds, then you should not try this move very often. Why try a certain tactic if you've already determined in advance that it probably won't show a profit? Game conditions change, though, and sometimes quickly and often. Be alert when players leave one of those three seats and are replaced by new players.

Structure Your Learning

Assignment #11

Next time you play in your regular game, perform the exercise of selecting a player in the big blind that you're going to victimize. Keep track of every time you raise to steal the blinds. Remember that your success is largely a function of the personality of the victim you've chosen and not necessarily attributable to the cards you hold.

Now here's the twist: Record the percentage of the time that you were successful in your records–under that player's name! Perform this exercise every time you play when you have enough time and opportunity, hopefully with a different player in the "hotseat." Do it long enough, and eventually you'll have a "Blind Stealing" index on most of your regular opponents.

Of all the poker tactics you could learn, stealing the blinds is one that's positively worth your time and effort to master. It's easy to understand, it's easy to pull off, it adds significantly to your hourly rate, it builds your confidence while you're learning other aspects of the game, and it doesn't require any special tools or equipment. But don't tell anyone I told you so.

Incidentally, if you play in a public cardroom and you want to know a player's name without drawing undue attention to yourself or the reason for your curiosity, there are several things you can do. You can introduce yourself to him, and he will usually give you his name in return. You can pay attention to the table talk and see if anyone at the table calls him by name. As a last resort, you can discreetly ask the floorman, who probably got his name before he seated him in the game.

16

THE SCIENCE OF TELLS

A **tell** is a clue that a player provides about his poker hand by the way he acts. The tell can be verbal or nonverbal, made unconsciously or knowingly, and genuine or part of a deliberate act.

General Advice

Before I get into specific tells, there are a few guidelines that apply whenever you see a tell and you're trying to analyze it:

1. At the lower limit games, where most of the players aren't too sophisticated, popular belief holds that the best way to fool the other players is to act weak when you're strong and act strong when you're weak. It's very common to see players who have a full house act like they can't even beat ace-high and players who can't even beat ace-high act like they have a full house.

For this reason I'll advise you, if you're going to act at all, to act like your hand is strong when it's strong and to act like it's weak when it's weak. Many of your opponents will think you're lying, because that's what they would do, and they'll often misread your hand.

2. If you're trying to figure out what a possible tell means, don't make things harder than they have to be. If you think the other player doesn't know that he just gave you a tell, you can go with what it usually means. If you think he's acting and he gave you that tell on purpose, you can proceed from there accordingly.

3. If you spot a tell and you honestly can't decide what it means, you have several options. You can stop the action, think about it until you arrive at a conclusion, and then make your play. Alternatively, you can ignore it completely and rely on the other information you have to help you evaluate the hand.

Chances are, if you can't decide what a tell means after reading this chapter, it's probably not that valuable to you. The best you can do is remember the tell, remember the cards the player had when you spotted his tell, make a note of it, and think about it after the game.

4. A player's general demeanor during the play of a hand is a big clue as to the strength of his hand. If he appears to be happy, enthusiastic, and not worried, he probably has a good hand. If he appears to be unhappy, acts disgusted with his hand, or makes negative remarks, he probably has a bad hand. His general demeanor won't tell you exactly what his hand is, but it's certainly one more bit of information that you can consider when making your decisions.

THE SCIENCE OF TELLS

Specific Tells

There are a number of tells that you might see during the course of a game. They covered in more depth in my first book, *Winner's Guide to Texas Hold'em Poker*, in Mike Caro's fantastic book *Caro's Book of Poker Tells* and in its companion video, *Caro's Pro Poker Tells*—all available from Cardoza Publishing.

What follows is a list of those tells with a brief explanation of each one. What I've characterized as "tells" include both specific mannerisms and general personality types. To help you develop a feel for the relative value of each one, I've rated each tell for you using the following scale:

> *-you won't see it often, has little value
> **-occurs often enough to help your hourly rate
> ***-common tell, worth knowing, good value
> ****-high frequency, very reliable, high value

1. *Impatience.* ** A player who is in a hurry to play his hand usually has a decent hand. It won't be a great hand, though, because a player holding A♦ A♥ or K♥ K♣ will usually wait until it's his turn to act to let anything be known about his hand.

2. *Mannerism changes.* ** Players who suddenly sit up in their chairs, put out their cigarettes, quickly finish their drinks, abruptly end conversations, or summarily dismiss any spectators usually have very good hands. You don't have to do any of these things if you intend to fold when it's your turn.

3. *Showing a hand to a spectator.* ✱✱ A player who shows his hand to a non-player when play begins usually has a good starting hand. A player who shows his hand to a non-player at the end of a hand, particularly when all of the cards are out and he is awaiting a call from a lone opponent, usually has a bad hand. Showing it is an effort to convince the other player that he's proud of his hand. When you see this tell, the bettor is usually betting as a stone cold bluff.

4. *First play by a good player.* ✱✱✱ Good players like to win the first hand they voluntarily enter the pot with, so they can then play with "your" money instead of theirs. Keep an eye on the player who usually doesn't play when he's in the small blind. If he does call in the small blind, he has a very good hand.

5. *Staring at the flop.* ✱✱✱✱ Players who continue to stare at the flop after the dealer turns it up usually did not flop anything. There's nothing there for them and it takes a few more seconds to double check it and make sure.

6. *Seeing the flop and quickly looking away.* ✱✱✱✱ If you hold 6♥ 6♣, and the flop is A♣ K♠ 10♥, the flop is easy to read even if you still have to take an extra second or two to make sure you've read it correctly. If you hold A♥ A♣, however, and the flop is 9♦ A♠ 3♥, it will look like this to you:

When you see this, you'll know instantly that you're going to bet. You'll quickly glance at your chips to make sure they're still there, and then you'll look away from the table, feigning total disinterest in the hand.

7. *Covering one's mouth.* ✱✱ A player who covers his mouth after betting is usually bluffing. What you're seeing is a conflict between the external physical action of betting and the internal knowledge of knowing you're "lying."

8. *Betting in a flamboyant style.* ✱✱ A player who throws his chips into the pot in a forceful or obviously exaggerated manner is usually bluffing. At the very least, he's trying to intimidate you into checking into him on the next round.

9. *Making directed bets.* ✱✱✱ A player who calls a bet by throwing his chips in the specific direction of a particular player (usually the bettor) is trying to intimidate the bettor into checking on the next round.

10. *Staring at other players.* ✱✱✱ This tell occurs most often after the river card comes and a player has missed a big draw. He will often noticeably raise his head from looking down at the flop, turn it to the left or right to face his sole opponent squarely, and then stare right at him. In poker language, this move means, "I just missed my flush draw. I'm entitled to win this hand, but I can't call a bet. Don't you dare bet into me."

11. *Calling your bet immediately.* ✳✳✳ A player who calls your bet and has his chips in the pot almost before you do has a weak calling hand. He'd rather you hadn't bet. Since you did, he wants his apparently quick and easy call to cause you to have second thoughts about betting into him on the next round.

12. *Reaching for chips to call your bet before you can make it.* ✳✳✳1/2 In poker language, this move means, "Of course I'm going to call your bet! It's such an easy decision for me that I don't even have to think about it. If you were betting to eliminate me, you can save that bet, since you can see that I'm going to call."

13. *Delaying in calling your bet.* ✳✳1/2 A player who genuinely couldn't decide between folding and calling when you bet on the flop is more likely to fold if he does call and you bet again on the turn. He usually will have been looking for a miracle card, took one shot at it, and is willing to fold on the turn if he misses (which will happen most of the time).

14. *Flashing one hole card.* ✳✳1/2 A player who makes sure you "accidentally" see one of his hole cards is bluffing. He almost never has what he wants you to think he does.

15. *Behavior on fabulous-looking flops.* ✳✳ Whenever the flop contains a high pair, three straight flush cards, or even three of a kind, you should pause a second before acting on your hand. A player who threw away

a hand with a card that would fit well with the flop will often let it be known.

How? Well, he might curse, moan, pound the table, slap his forehead, elbow his neighbor, or actually announce out loud what card he folded before the flop. You have to wait to give him a second to do one of these things. This is a very reliable tell since a player not in the hand has no reason to influence its play or outcome.

16. *Unnecessarily showing the nuts at the end.* ✳1/2 A player who does this might just be bragging, but sometimes it's because he intends to bluff you in the near future and he wants you to remember that he only plays the nuts.

17. *Coaxing along an opponent's end decision.* ✳ Let's say a player bets into you, and you're slowly and reluctantly about to fold. It's apparent that you're about to exit the hand, and your opponent says or does something to help you confirm that you're making the "right" decision. He's bluffing. He wants you to hurry up and fold before you take a second to rethink what you're doing.

18. *Showing visible disappointment.* ✳✳✳✳ With a very big pot, if a player is on a draw to the nuts and misses on the end, he will often let you know about it. Again, the secret is that you have to wait a second for him to do it. He might exhale deeply, slump down in his chair, curse, look sad, turn his cards face up as a gesture of folding, throw his cards into the muck out of turn, hit the table, or tell you what hand he missed.

19. *Rabbit hunting.* ✳✳✳ Rabbit hunting is the term for, "Can I see the next card, please?" after the hand is over. It seems that bad players like to do that and good players don't.

20. *Neat and conservative players.* ✳✳1/2 A person's style of doing one thing is usually also his style of doing most other things. A player who dresses and acts conservatively usually also plays conservatively.

21. *Players in wheelchairs and walkers.* ✳✳ Players who are wheelchair-bound or otherwise have physical trouble getting around like to stay put once they get in the game. They usually play conservatively but not excellently. They're generally Tight/Passive players.

How to Be Tell-Less

1. *Get into a routine.* Make sure you are familiar with all of the tells mentioned in this chapter, and think about how you look to the other players. Try to do the same thing every time you bet. In advance, think about the physical actions that you go through when you bet or check and try t to keep your behavior uniform.

2. *Be prepared.* Often your opponent will actually ask you what your hand is or what your hole cards are. My reply is always the same, and said with a smile: "I don't remember."

You can also deflect the question with one of your own: "What do you think I have?"

3. *Use time to your advantage.* When you get your cards, wait until it's your turn to look at them. When the flop comes, spend that time watching other players watch the flop, especially if there was a preflop raiser.

4. *Watch your table talk.* Don't talk about the hands you've played, the hands you've folded, or why you did or didn't play a hand a certain way. Don't show your hands if you're not called.

Back in 1985, when my son Neil was six-years-old, he and I were playing head-up no-limit hold'em at the kitchen table. During one hand he made a pot-sized bet, and I folded. After I threw my cards in the muck I asked him, "What do you have?" He had a stack of chips in front of him that was so high that I could barely see him sitting behind them. He raised himself up so that I could see his eyes peering out from behind that stack, shook his head from side to side and said, "Oh, no. You got to pay to see 'em."

Structure Your Learning
Assignment #12
If possible, get a copy of *Caro's Book of Poker Tells* and the *Pro Poker Tells* video. You can find the book in most bookstores. You can also buy the book and the video directly from Cardoza Publishing, which you

can reach by phone at 1-800-577-WINS, or on the Internet at www.cardozabooks.com.

So many low limit players are unaware of the science of tells, and the average low-limit game is rich with them. Once you learn how to recognize the most common tells and how to profit from them, you will have even greater results than you do now.

Poker is actually a game of people played with cards, not a game of cards played with people. The player who accepts and understands this fact and works to take advantage of it will be way ahead of the player who doesn't.

PLAYING WITH AN ACE

About 15% of the time, one of your hole cards will be an ace. That's about one out of every seven hands, six times per hour, or fifty times per eight-hour playing session that you'll be dealt an ace with another random card. It's very important that you learn to play correctly when you have an ace, as this one aspect of the game alone has a huge effect on your hourly rate.

If you're in a certain situation as many as six times per hour, and you have a chance to put as many as four or more big bets into play each time, then you can see what an impact playing your aces correctly can have on your hourly rate. When you're betting as many as twenty-four big bets per hour, you'd better know what you're doing if your long-term goal is to win one to two big bets per hour.

Here's the golden rule of playing with an ace: *Every other player at the table also gets an ace one out of six hands. Getting an ace is no big deal, so there has to be something special about yours.* Following are two tables of ace-related odds that will be helpful to you:

ODDS THAT YOU WILL BE DEALT	
At least one ace	5.7-1
AK (not suited)	110-1
AK (suited)	331-1
AA	221-1

PERCENTAGE CHANCE THAT NO ONE HOLDS AN ACE BEFORE THE FLOP	
In a ten-handed game	13.3%
If you do (ten-handed)	25.3%
If you don't (ten-handed)	15.6%
In a five-handed game	41.3%
If you do (five-handed)	58.6%
If you don't (five-handed)	48.6%

Looking at this second table, you can see that in a ten-handed game, someone will be dealt an ace 86.7% of the time, if you have an ace, another player will also have one 74.7% of the time, and if you don't have an ace, someone else will have one 84.4% of the time. You see the importance of playing your aces correctly.

PLAYING WITH AN ACE

Most low limit players see the flop every time they have an ace in their hand. Most low limit players are also losers in the long run, and I can tell you that this incorrect play of aces is one of the reasons. A player who learns to play his aces correctly will have fixed a big leak in his game. With an opportunity to make an expensive mistake as often as once every six hands, it is positively worth your time and effort to learn to play correctly.

If you're one of those players who likes to play every ace, and you're looking to improve your game a little bit without too much work, the best advice I can give you is: don't play your ace unless your other card is either a 10 or higher or the same suit as your ace. This will plug a big leak in your game and help keep you out of trouble if you're presently playing more hands.

For those of you who'd like to fine-tune your game a little more than that, keep reading, because this chapter offers much more specific advice. I'm going to take the A♠, pair it up with every other card in the deck, and give you a brief comment about the resulting hand.

You don't have to agree with everything I say about these hands. How you play a hand depends on the situation you're facing when it's your turn to act. A correct play in one instance might not be best the next time you have that same hand. My main purpose in this exercise is to make you think about your aces, so you don't automatically play all of them every time.

A♠ A♣, A♠ A♥, A♠ A♦. Always raise and reraise before the flop with these hands.

A♠ K♠, A♠ K♣, A♠ K♥, A♠ K♦. Raise in early position and just call in late position unless you're raising to steal the blinds.

A♠ Q♠, A♠ Q♣, A♠ Q♥, A♠ Q♦. Same play as with the kings, except you don't have to play the hand at all if you have to call three or more bets cold. That raise and reraise ahead of you mean something–probably that someone has pocket aces, kings or AK.

A♠ J♠, A♠ J♣, A♠ J♥, A♠ J♦. These hands are usually best if there's no preflop raise, or if you're short-handed. Being suited helps but not until you see the flop.

A♠ 10♠, A♠ 10♣, A♠ 10♥, A♠ 10♦. At least you can make the nut straight using both cards, which is a big plus.

A♠ 9♠, A♠ 9♣, A♠ 9♥, A♠ 9♦. A 9 kicker is about as low as I will play in most instances. If another player in the hand has an ace, his kicker will almost always be bigger than mine.

A♠ 8♠, A♠ 7♠, A♠ 6♠, A♠ 5♠, A♠ 4♠, A♠ 3♠, A♠ 2♠. Although these hands are all suited, they don't have much value until you see the flop. You will flop two more spades only 10.944% of the time, which is about one out of nine times. You need to be playing in late position or have a lot of other players in the hand to have the right odds to see the flop. You can, though, raise to steal the blinds with these hands.

A♠ 5♣, A♠ 5♥, A♠ 5♦. If you absolutely must play an ace with a garbage card, this is the one to pick. Why? Because you can make a wheel using both hole cards. A5 doesn't win many hands, but it's worth more money to you than A6 because of its straight potential.

A♠ 8♣, A♠ 8♥, A♠ 8♦, A♠ 7♣, A♠ 7♥, A♠ 7♦, A♠ 6♣, A♠ 6♥, A♠ 6♦, A♠ 4♣, A♠ 4♥, A♠ 4♦, A♠ 3♣, A♠ 3♥, A♠ 3♦, A♠ 2♣, A♠ 2♥, A♠ 2♦. These are all of the other hands with an ace. They are all garbage hands, and you should play them only in the blinds or perhaps when you're stealing the blinds. If you follow my advice, these will be the hands that the other players will be holding when you beat them.

There's one other time when you might think about playing an ace with a bad kicker–when the jackpot for your game is very high and it takes aces full or better to be beaten to qualify. Statistically speaking, it's likely that the winning hand will contain exactly one ace more than any other card. Let's look at an example:

You hold A♦ 6♥, the board is A♥ A♣ J♠ 9♦ A♠, and another player holds K♠ K♣, Q♥ Q♦, or J♥ J♣.
That's a jackpot in most cardrooms in the country. You have four aces, and your opponent has a full

house–aces full of kings, queens or jacks. In most places, the loser must play both hole cards, and the winner must play only one hole card. In some places, the winner's kicker must beat the board, which is a stupid rule because it means you're using six cards to make up your poker hand. In most places, though, the winner's kicker is irrelevant.

Since, as you can see, all you need is an ace in your hand to win the jackpot, many players will play every time they have an ace for that reason. A jackpot gets hit this way only once in about 12,500 hands, so you'll have to know the size of your jackpot and decide for yourself if it's worth it.

This calculation also assumes that you're the one to hit the jackpot. Consider this question: "Is the jackpot big enough to make up for all those ace hands that I lose with while I'm trying to hit it?"

It's impossible to answer this question precisely, because there are so many variables that cannot be quantified. My advice is that you don't play aces solely for the jackpot unless all three of these conditions are met:

1. The jackpot is over $15,000.
2. You're playing at a full table.
3. You are a solid, experienced player.

See Chapter 20 for a more detailed explanation.

PLAYING WITH AN ACE

I can tell you that in all the years I've been playing hold'em, I've been a winner in a jackpot hand three times. The first time, I held A♣ A♥, made four aces, and beat a player who made four kings with K♠ K♣. The other two times I held A♥ K♥ and A♣ Q♦, respectively, when three more aces came on the board, and the other player had a big pocket pair. Holding a single ace has helped me win a jackpot only twice in twenty years, and I think my experience is typical.

My personal philosophy regarding aces and jackpots is to forget completely that the two are related. I play my cards based on their poker value, and I don't worry about the jackpot. I've never thrown away a hand like A♦ 7♣ that would have won the jackpot if I'd played it. Let the jackpot take care of itself; devote your mental energy to the more profitable aspects of the game.

Structure Your Learning
Assignment #13
Nothing in this short chapter was exceedingly difficult to learn. I just want you to think about those hands that have an ace in them.

Your assignment, therefore, is to make a list of those hands with an ace that you used to play but, after reading this chapter, have now decided not to play. Every time you throw away one of these hands before the flop, record the outcome of the hand. All you want to know is whether you would have won the hand. I'm betting that most of the time the answer will be "No."

STRADDLES, KILLS, AND OVERS

Straddles, kills, and overs are related because they affect the structure and limit of the game you're playing. When you take a seat in a $3/$6 or a $1/$4/$8/$8 game, you know what the limits are, and you have an idea of how much it would cost to play each hand to its conclusion. You therefore also know what an appropriate buy-in is for that game.

Playing the overs or playing with a straddle or a kill increases the limits. All of these plays require you to invest more money in the hand than you might originally have intended to when you sat down in the game. That in turn means that you might be busted out of the game before you realize it. Let's look at each one of these subjects separately.

Playing With A Straddle
A **straddle** is when the player to the immediate left of the big blind raises **in the dark** (before he gets his cards). In most cardrooms, this blind raise does not

count toward the maximum raise limit, so, if your cardroom has a three raise limit, you'll be playing with a bet and four raises if there's a straddle. With one possible exception, you should never straddle the pot yourself. Take a minute here to see if you can think of what that exception might be.

Got it yet? This is one instance where it's useful to think outside the game. The one time you should straddle concerns your image. If you're in a game full of loose, wild players who are playing and straddling almost every hand, you should also straddle the blind once in a while. You don't want to stand out as a tight, conservative, no-action rock, especially in light of all that action going on around you.

The one extra bet that it costs you to straddle is really more of an investment than an actual bet. If you get into the spirit of the game and appear to be one of the loose players, the pots that you win in the future will have more bets in them, on average, than they would if the other players perceived you as a too-tight player.

If you've decided you're going to straddle, the most important thing you need to know is: *do it as soon as you can after you've made the decision.* You only have to do it once or twice so that the other players can see it and think that you're just playing for fun. The earlier in the game that you straddle a hand or two, the more time there will be for you to take advantage of your looser image.

STRADDLES, KILLS, AND OVERS

It's very important that you don't complain about the straddling or in any way let others know that you don't like it. Don't let your words or demeanor contradict your actions on the subject of straddling. Try to look happy, and don't give your opponents anything to doubt your (fake) image, as a Loose/Passive player.

When one of the other players has straddled, here's what you need to consider:

1. The straddler will have a random hand since he raised before he saw his hand.

2. The raise has reduced your implied odds, and you don't know what the straddler has, so you should play only your very good hands.

3. If you do have a playable hand, you should think about coming in for a reraise. That would make it three bets to go for the players behind you, which helps increase the chance that you'll get head-up with the straddler. Your good hand against the straddler's random hand, plus the fact that you have position on him, all make you a big favorite to win the hand.

4. If another player reraises behind you, he probably has a great hand and is raising to eliminate players.

5. You just can't steal the blinds in this situation. Who's going to straddle and then fold when you reraise? Most of the time the straddler is going to reraise you just because you raised. You're always going to have to take a flop here so remember that ahead of time.

Playing With A Kill

A **kill** game is a little different than playing with a straddle. It's specifically advertised as a kill game in advance, so it's usually full of good players who occasionally like to play higher limit. A kill game has tougher players than the same limit game without the kill, on average.

The kill is activated by one of two circumstances:

1. The same player wins two hands in a row. When that happens, the next game is played at the kill limit, usually double the original stakes.

2. A player wins a pot that's bigger than a predetermined limit, usually ten times the size of the big bet. The next hand is played at the kill limit.

In each case, the player who won the pot, called the "Killer," posts a big blind twice the size of the usual big blind, regardless of his position at the table. If you were playing $3/$6 and you were the Killer, you'd post a blind of $6 instead of $3, and the game would be played at the $6/$12 limit. If a different player wins the kill hand, or the pot is not big enough to trigger a kill, the next hand reverts to the original game limit.

STRADDLES, KILLS, AND OVERS

When a player wins a hand, he is said to "have a leg up." To show this, the dealer gives him a button that says, "Leg Up" on one side. This helps everyone remember and identify him as the winner of the last hand. If he wins the next hand, he turns the button over, revealing its second side, where it says, "Killer."

If you have a leg up, you have to ask yourself this question: "Do I, or do I not, want to win this next hand so we can play a kill game with me as the Killer?" I think you should lean towards wanting a kill game if you can meet two of the four following criteria:

1. You're slated to be in the big blind the next hand anyway. In this case you can kill for only an extra $3 instead of the full $6.

2. You're in late position. Players tend to call less often before the flop in kill games, which in turn makes a late position steal raise more likely to be successful.

3. The game is short-handed. With few players, a raise from the Killer will give almost everyone the wrong odds to play. If you also happen to be in late position, or even in the small blind, a raise is a good move.

4. You're one of the best players in the game. It's impossible to cover every conceivable situation in a book this size. But if you're a great hold'em player, or at least one of the best in the game, you'll know how to outplay your opponents. Playing for twice the usual stakes will be all the better for you.

This advice applies only if you have a truly undecided hand when you have a leg up. If you have A♣ A♥ or 7♦ 2♥, you'll know instantly what you want to do. It's those hands in the middle that you have to think about. So know yourself. Do what you think will work best for you. If you're really undecided, throw the hand away. Don't bet that you know what you're doing when you really don't.

Playing The Overs

Playing the overs is the term for an agreement made between certain players at the table to play for a higher limit when only they are in the hand. Overs players get a button from the dealer identifying them as such. They have to keep this button in front of them, and if they change their minds about wanting to play the overs, they flip it to its second side, where it says, "No."

Here's how this situation works: Assume you're playing $1/$5 hold'em and there are a few players in the game who'd like to play $1/$20. Those players get overs buttons, and when the last non-overs player drops out of the hand, the limit immediately goes up to $20 for the overs players still left in the hand.

If you don't want to play the overs, this rule will never affect you. You'll never have to play anything except the $1-$5 game you sat down in. So you really shouldn't object when other players in your game want to play the overs.

If you do decide to become an overs player, here are a few things to keep in mind:

1. Play a little tighter than usual. If you're new at overs play, the other players are obviously more experienced at it than you are. Limit the number of hands you call with to see the flop. This will reduce your exposure to the better players while you're learning the game.

2. Remember that you're really playing a higher limit game. Drawing hands, low suited connectors and low pocket pairs go down in value in an overs game.

3. Don't unnecessarily drive out the last non-overs player if you don't want to play the rest of the hand for the higher stakes. Think ahead.

Structure Your Learning
Assignment #14
This chapter is mainly just for your information. You probably don't play in too many games where you have to worry about straddles, kills and overs. You probably see a straddle more than any of the others, and I want you to be able to analyze the situation objectively when necessary.

However, when you feel that you are a good enough hold'em player, I want you to seek out aggressively and play in a kill game or an overs game where you can agree on an overs limit that satisfies you. If you have to, work it out in advance away from the poker room with a fellow hold'em player who would also like to play the overs. There's nothing wrong with telling anyone why you're doing this, which is to play occasionally and safely in a higher limit game in an effort to improve. Don't forget to record your results in your record book. Good luck!

SPREAD LIMIT

Spread limit is a betting structure that allows you to bet any amount between a preset minimum and maximum. The most common spread limit hold'em game is $1-$5. Sometimes you'll see a $2-$10 hold'em game, although $2-$10 is more often used in a 7-Card Stud game. Here's a list of things you need to know if you're going to play in a spread limit game:

1. Most of the hands you play will be short-handed, and there will be more folding after the flop than in a structured game. Players know that they're not getting the good implied odds they need to chase draws.

2. If it's a passive game (one without much raising), you can limp in for $1 quite often with weak and speculative hands to see if you hit the flop. If you miss, it costs you only $1. If you hit, you'll make more than enough to make up for your misses.

3. There are no free cards to buy, and semi-bluffing isn't very common, since bets don't double on the turn.

4. You should raise more to protect big pairs and big cards. Use the tactic of check-raising if you can.

5. It's harder to chase players out as the pots get bigger. Since the maximum bet is only $5, each $5 that goes into the pot after that is a smaller fraction of the pot than the previous bet was.

For example, calling a $5 bet when the pot contains $15 means you are getting pot odds of 3-1. You might fold your hand with odds that low. Calling that same $5 bet when there's $50 in the pot means you're getting pot odds of 10-1. Now you're almost trapped into calling because of the pot odds.

6. If you have a weak or speculative hand, and it's raised behind you, you should usually fold if you have only $1 invested in the hand.

7. There are a lot of bad players in spread limit games. What makes them bad is that they don't understand game theory. One of the most glaring mistakes that they routinely make is to bet less than the maximum with good hands. This error gives their opponents the right odds to run them down, where the opponents couldn't even call if they'd bet the maximum.

8. There's another popular mistake that these bad players make. When they raise before the flop, they often choose an amount to raise that they think is indicative of the value of their hand. In other words, such

an opponent might raise only $1 with pocket 2s, 3s, and 4s. He might raise $2 with pocket 5s, 6s and 7s. He might raise $3 with 8s, 9s, and 10s, and $5 with his highest pairs. These players give away too much information without charging the maximum amount they can for it.

Structure Your Learning

Assignment #15

The next time you have to play in a spread limit game, prepare yourself by rereading this chapter. If you play in a public poker room, you probably have the option of playing 7-Card Stud while you're waiting to get in the hold'em game, and it's probably a $1-$5 stud game. Think about what you learned in this chapter that can be applied to stud. It can only help.

JACKPOTS

There are two ways that the average low limit hold'em player can score a big win in the game. One way is to win or place high in a hold'em tournament. The other way is to hit a jackpot. You hit a jackpot by making a very good hand, such as A♠ A♣ A♥ J♦ J♣, and then losing with it! Actually, it will look like this:

You hold	The board is	Another player holds
J♠ J♣	A♠ A♣ A♥ 9♦ 5♣	A♦ Q♥

You have a full house (aces full of jacks), and your opponent has four aces. You also must fulfill six other criteria with this hand:

1. You made the minimum high hand required, which is aces full of jacks or better (so this would also work if you held pocket queens or kings).

2. There were four or more players dealt into the hand.

3. There was a minimum of $20 or $30 in the pot, depending on the poker room rules.

4. You, as the loser of the hand, are playing both of your hole cards.

5. The winner of the hand has made four of a kind, or better.

6. The winner's kicker beats the board.

Before I go any further, I want to make a few comments about jackpots that I find very important. Any time there is money involved in something, there's the possibility of its misuse, abuse and plain ol' outright theft. Here are a few things that I want you to know about jackpots:

1. The money that goes into a jackpot pool comes from the players. $1 from every hand played that reaches a certain threshold is taken out of the pot and set aside for the jackpot. It's your money! It does not belong to the casino or the poker room. It is not the property of the poker room manager. Casino management cannot touch it. The money in the jackpot is a side bet among the players, collected $1 at a time.

2. Jackpot money has, all too often, been very mismanaged. When the Grand Casinos opened in Biloxi and Gulfport, Mississippi, they had jackpots. They also had a notice on the poker room wall that they were taking a "15% administrative fee" out of the jackpot for the costs of administering it (including counting the jackpot money, physically protecting it, and doing the paperwork associated with it).

Over the course of several years, they took thousands of dollars from the players, before the Mississippi Gaming Commission ruled that they could not continue to operate that way. In actuality, this money probably helped defray the costs of running the poker room, which is what the rake is designed to do. So, the way I see it, those players were getting raked twice.

Another incident happened when the Bayou Caddy Jubilee, in Lakeshore, Mississippi, closed its poker room while there were still tens of thousands of dollars in the poker jackpot. They took that money from the poker players and used it to inflate the size of some jackpots on selected slot machines. In other words, they took the poker players' money and gave it to the slot players. A group of poker players sued them over this incident; I don't know how the case was decided.

3. Some poker rooms make the jackpot exceedingly difficult to hit. They require that four of a kind or better be beaten by a higher four of a kind or better. The odds against this happening, especially if both players have to use both of their hole cards, are astronomical. So why do they do it?

Because they're greedy, that's why. When the requirements to hit the jackpot are ridiculously out of sight, it takes years for the jackpot to get hit. Meanwhile, the jackpot grows steadily, and the poker room management uses its size to attract more players. This way, they ensure that they have plenty of games to rake, which in turn ensures that the poker room makes a profit for management.

The poker room manager looks good to his bosses, and he's using your money to do so. When a jackpot takes several years to go over $100,000, who do you think is collecting the bank interest on that money? I promise you it's not you.

4. Some poker rooms have a rule that says they can take the $1 jackpot drop when the pot reaches $20, but the players are not eligible to hit the jackpot until the pot reaches $30. This means that if there is between $20 and $29 in the pot, you can't win the jackpot if it's hit even though you've already paid the $1.

Why does this rule exist? I've asked around and no one will give me a good answer. Logic tells me, therefore, that it's a device that poker room management uses to keep a jackpot from being hit as often.

It probably works, too, because at the lower limits a big portion of the pots are going to be between $20 and $29. It keeps the jackpot amount big, so they can use it to attract players. I believe it's probably an illegal rule, because it requires you to pay for something that you can't get. Imagine playing a slot machine with a progressive jackpot, always playing the maximum number of coins so you qualify for the jackpot, and when you finally hit it, having management tell you that you can't have the jackpot because it's not big enough yet!

5. Another jackpot rule I don't like is the requirement that a certain minimum number of players, usually four, be dealt in the hand to qualify for the jackpot. Why can't two or three players play for the jackpot? This rule is based on management's ignorance of the jackpot odds; I'll explain why shortly. It's completely arbitrary and not based on anything substantial.

6. There's also the rule that says the winner's hole cards must both play. This means that in the case of four aces, the winner's kicker must be higher than any other card on the board. It's a bad rule that probably wouldn't withstand a Gaming Commission challenge, because it requires you to play six cards to make up your poker hand.

Why does the rule exist? To make it harder to hit the jackpot, and therefore to keep the jackpot big, so the poker room can use it to attract more players to play in games that they can rake.

7. The last rule that I have a problem with is the one that says that if the game is a little short-handed, and the players want a reduced rake, they then can't play for the jackpot. In other words, the poker room manager will say, "Yes, you can play with a reduced rake (usually just $1 maximum), but then you're ineligible for the jackpot."

Of all the rules related to jackpots, this one's the worst. In my opinion, it's nothing but a scam that the poker room knowingly perpetrates upon the players. Why? Because there's absolutely no relationship between the amount of money that the house rakes to meet its expenses and the side bet that the players make among themselves to put into a jackpot pool.

The jackpot money comes from the players and belongs to the players. It's held in trust by the poker room for the players, and only a player can win any of that money. It is not related to anything else that goes on in the poker room.

So why does the poker room management tell you that the rake and the jackpot are connected? Again, it's because they're greedy. They know that most players will want to play for a jackpot if there is one. Most players, when told that they can't play for that jackpot if the rake is reduced, will change their minds and say, "Go ahead and leave the rake where it is. We don't want to hit the jackpot and not win it just because we're a little short-handed."

Jackpot Odds

There is no way to know the exact odds of hitting a jackpot. Have you ever been in a game where someone said after the hand was over, "We would have hit the jackpot if I hadn't thrown my hand away before the flop?" That's why you can never know the exact odds of hitting a jackpot. You cannot account for the actions of all the players with mathematical certainty.

JACKPOTS

All you can know for sure is that the more players there are in the game who see every flop, especially when they're holding an ace, the more likely it is that you'll eventually hit a jackpot. On the other hand, it will take a very long time to hit a jackpot if you're in a very tight game where hardly anyone ever sees the flop, and most hands don't go past it.

The only way to know the approximate odds of hitting a jackpot is to use hindsight, and that's what I have done. The poker room managers of three different casinos have given me access to their hold'em jackpot histories.

This is not privileged, classified, nor secret information. This information is available to anyone who cares to keep an eye on the jackpots and record how much each jackpot was when it was hit. If you also know how each jackpot dollar is distributed (75%-15%-10% or 67%-33%), you can calculate how many hands were dealt, on average, between jackpot hands.

I have ten years of statistics from three poker rooms, for a total of thirty years of hold'em records. It turns out that the magic number is 12,500. That's how many hands it takes, on average, to hit a jackpot. This takes into account loose play, tight play, players who play every ace, players who only play aces selectively, the play of small pocket pairs and all the other variables that can't be calculated in advance.

Knowing that it takes 12,500 hands to hit a jackpot is not really the whole story. Assuming the table is full, every time a hand is dealt, there will be forty-five individual hand matchups. In a ten-handed game, all of the players at the table can match up all of their hands a total of forty-five different ways. So you can see this more clearly, I'll list for you just how each hand can match up with the others:

1. The player in the first seat can match up his hand with the players in seats 2, 3, 4, 5, 6, 7, 8, 9, and 10, for a total of nine matchups. TOTAL: 9

2. The player in the second seat can match up his hand with the players in seats 3, 4, 5, 6, 7, 8, 9, and 10, for a total of eight matchups. TOTAL: 9 + 8 = 17

3. The player in the third seat can match up his hand with the players in seats 4, 5, 6, 7, 8, 9, and 10, for a total of seven matchups. TOTAL: 9 + 8 + 7 = 24

4. The player in the fourth seat can match up his hand with the players in seats 5, 6, 7, 8, 9, and 10, for a total of six matchups. TOTAL: 9 + 8 + 7 + 6 = 30

5. The player in the fifth seat can match up his hand with the players in seats 6, 7, 8, 9, and 10, for a total of five matchups. TOTAL: 9 + 8 + 7 + 6 + 5 = 35

6. The player in the sixth seat can match up his hand with the players in seats 7, 8, 9, and 10, for a total of four matchups. TOTAL: 9 + 8 + 7 + 6 +5 + 4 = 39

7. The player in the seventh seat can match up his hand with the players in seats 8, 9, and 10, for a total of three matchups. TOTAL: 9 + 8 + 7 + 6 + 5 + 4 + 3 = 42

8. The player in the eighth seat can match up his hand with the players in seats 9 and 10, for a total of two matchups. TOTAL: 9 + 8 + 7 + 6 + 5 + 4 + 3 + 2 = 44

9. The player in the ninth seat can match up his hand with the player in the tenth seat for only one matchup. Total: 9 + 8 + 7 + 6 + 5 + 4 + 3 + 2 + 1 = 45

This list means that for every hand dealt, there are forty-five hand matchups. If it takes 12,500 hands to hit a jackpot, then when a jackpot is hit, on average, there will have been a total of 562,500 hand matchups (12,500 x 45 = 562,500). That number applies for a full, ten-handed game.

If the games were all nine-handed, then there would be only thirty-six matchups per hand, and you would have to divide 562,500 by 36 to get the number of hands that it would take to hit the jackpot. That comes out to be 15,625 hands (562,500/36 = 15,625).

With just one player fewer at a table, the odds against hitting the jackpot increase by exactly 25% (12,500 + 25% = 15,625) instead of 10% as you might expect. That's because the number of possible matchups decreases exponentially as each player leaves the game.

Using the above math as a foundation, I've created the following table to tell you the odds against hitting a jackpot with various numbers of players in the game.

ODDS AGAINST HITTING A JACKPOT			
total # of players	matchups	divided by # matchups	# hands needed to hit jackpot
10	562,500	45	12,500
9	562,500	36	15,625
8	562,500	28	20,089
7	562,500	21	26,785
6	562,500	15	37,500
5	562,500	10	56,250
4	562,500	6	93,750
3	562,500	3	187,500
2	562,500	1	562,500

Notice that if the game is only half-full, the odds against hitting the jackpot more than quadruple, rather than just double. This table also shows why (if the game is very short-handed), you should not play for a small jackpot. With the game already short-handed, the pots will be much smaller than usual, and the $1 that's taken out for the jackpot will be a much larger percentage of the pot than usual.

You'll make more money in the long run if you leave that dollar in the pot where you can win it now.

JACKPOTS

Don't use that dollar to make a bet that you can beat the 56,000+ to 1 odds to get a share of the jackpot in the next few hours. If your game is five-handed and you're playing thirty-five hands per hour for the next three hours, then you'll have played 105 hands. 56,250/105=535.7. Your odds of hitting the jackpot in the next three hours are 535.7 to 1.

Would you rather have the extra $30 or so that you will win today by not playing for the jackpot, or would you rather give up that money in exchange for the long odds of hitting the jackpot? That $30 saved 535 times equals $16,071. Would your share of any jackpot be that big if you hit it? Usually not.

There's one other thing about jackpots that you should know. It concerns the Omaha jackpot, if there is one. My research has shown me that an Omaha jackpot is about four times easier to hit than a hold'em jackpot. Why? It's because there are more hand matchups in Omaha than there are in hold'em.

An Omaha player who is dealt A♣ J♣ 9♥ 7♥ doesn't have just one hand. He has six of them:

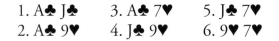

    1. A♣ J♣   3. A♣ 7♥   5. J♣ 7♥
    2. A♣ 9♥   4. J♣ 9♥   6. 9♥ 7♥

Just two Omaha players can matchup their hands in thirty-six different ways! It takes nine hold'em players to achieve that many matchups. How many times have you been in a hold'em game where one of the players had the minimum losing hand to hit the jackpot and no one beat him?

In an Omaha game, every player in the hand will have six times as many hands as he would in a hold'em game. Because of that, someone will beat him about four times as often as in the hold'em game. Why four times and not six times as often? Two reasons:

1. It's impossible for 2s, 3s and 4s to make a qualifying hand under most circumstances.

2. Some Omaha games require that the losing hand be four of a kind rather than just aces full.

What does this mean to you, and how do you take advantage of this information? Assuming you're going to let the jackpots be the deciding factor in your game selection, you should make sure to do the following:

1. When you enter the poker room and are deciding which games to play, look at the hold'em and Omaha jackpots. If the hold'em jackpot is more than four times as large as the Omaha jackpot, then you should play hold'em. Alternatively, if the Omaha jackpot is less than one-fourth as big as the hold'em jackpot, then you should still play hold'em.

2. Learn to play Omaha if you don't already know how. Assuming you are going to be a poker player in the broader sense of the term, and not just a hold'em

player, you should know how to play more than one poker game. As you can see, it's worth money to you. If you're interested in this topic, look for my book on Omaha that's due to be published about six months after this one.

3. Determine how many tables there are of each game, because the jackpot can be hit at only one table. For example, if the hold'em jackpot is $8,000 and the Omaha jackpot is $2,000, it's a mathematical toss-up whether to play hold'em or Omaha. If, however, there are two hold'em games going, and only one Omaha game going, that cuts your odds in half that you'll be at the right table when the hold'em jackpot is hit, and it clearly makes Omaha the better game.

4. If you're new to Omaha or you play but not that well, and you think the jackpot is worth playing for, ask the card room manager to start an Omaha game with the lowest limits that will still qualify for the jackpot. You can probably get a $2/$4 game going, especially if you let the other players in the room know what you're doing and why.

Don't forget that the money in the jackpot belongs to the players. You're the customer. If you're successful at getting this game started, the most important thing is that you make sure it is for high only, and not high-low split. High-low split is a game that requires a great deal of skill to play well, so those games are usually populated by experts.

Before I end this chapter, did I mention that the jackpot money belongs to the players and not to the poker room or casino management?

Structure Your Learning
Assignment #16
If you play in a poker room with jackpot rules that you don't like, talk to the poker room management about it. They do listen, and they do respond to players' comments. If you feel that a rule is especially egregious, and you can't get satisfaction from the poker room, consider making a complaint to the gaming commission. Your complaint may be just the one they're waiting for to take action.

If the jackpot influences you to do something you would not ordinarily have done, record that in your records. If you're lucky enough to hit and share in a jackpot, record the amount in your records as a win. For example, if you won $65 playing hold'em during your entire session, and you got another $350 as your share of a jackpot, you should record a win of $415 in your records. Be sure to mention the jackpot so you can explain the big win.

When you play and don't win the jackpot, the money that goes into the jackpot comes from you. It's a loss that you don't see, because your share of the jackpot drop might be as low as 10¢ per hand in a full game. The records you've been keeping up to this point include the loss of the jackpot drop, so it's only right that you count the win when you get some of it back.

JACKPOTS

You should know that some poker players are almost exclusively "jackpot chasers." They move from poker room to poker room and from game to game in an effort to play in the one game in town that has the best jackpot with the best odds of being hit. If you are going to focus on jackpots at all, I recommend that you follow their method. Your hourly rate will increase significantly if you can become one of these players. Good luck!

OVERCALLING

Overcalling is the term for calling a bet after another player or other players has/have already called that bet. For the purposes of this book, we'll be concerned only with the betting and calling that takes place on the river, after all of the cards are out. To overcall a bet on the river, there must already be a bet, and you can't be the first player to act after it. Before the action gets to you, one or more players must act on that bet for it to qualify as the subject of this discussion.

If you already have some experience playing hold'em in a live game, you probably know that the first player to bet on the river often does not have a good hand. He could have been on a draw, missed, and now be betting as a bluff. He may have a low pair, or even two pair, that he knows will not win if he checks. He might, however, have the nuts or some unexpected great hand. Sometimes you just can't know for sure what a bet from the first player really means.

One thing you do know for sure is that, even though the bettor could have anything, the first player to call him has to have something. If you're the next player after that first caller, you have some analytical thinking to do. First, you have to think about what kind of poker hand the original bettor has. Second, you have to think about what kind of hand the first caller thinks the bettor has. Since he called first, knowing that you're behind him and could possibly raise, you usually have to give him credit for a reasonably good hand.

You have to figure out why that player called. Does he have a lousy hand, can beat only a bluff, and is hoping you won't call? Is he calling with a fairly lousy hand, just because the pot is very big? Is he calling with a great hand (or even the nuts), just so you'll also call?

It also helps if you know the players in question. If that's the case, here are four easy questions that you can quickly ask yourself:

1. Are both the bettor and the caller extremely loose players? If so, then either of them could have anything, and if you're truly undecided, you should lean toward calling.

2. Is the bettor a loose player and the caller a tight player? If so, you can be sure that the caller has a good read on the bettor. He doesn't think he's throwing his money away in this spot. In this situation, you should fold if you're undecided.

3. Is the bettor a tight player and the caller a loose player? A tight player who is first to act is capable of bluffing in this spot. The loose player is capable of calling with anything in this spot. You should generally consider calling, unless you know for sure that the first player who bet just doesn't bluff in this spot or has a habit of checking his good hands.

4. Are the bettor and caller both tight players? If so, then you'll usually need a much better than average hand to call.

Just like playing loose is not always a bad tactic, playing tight is not always the best tactic. It's really a question of how good your opponents are. There's no substitute for knowing your opponents.

If you could know only the bettor or the caller, not both, you'd make the best decisions in the long run by knowing the caller. The first caller is the key player in this equation. If you recognize the caller as a good, solid, experienced player (and especially if you know that he's just a better overall player than you), you can take advantage of that knowledge.

Structure Your Learning
Assignment #17
The next time you play in your usual game, keep track of the times that you make an overcall on the river. Record how many big bets you win and how many you lose when you're in these situations. If you make

an overcall and lose the hand, count that as losing one big bet. If you make an overcall and win the hand, count the number of big bets in the pot, minus the bet you called with.

All you have to do is keep a running, cumulative total of big bets won and lost. You're not concerned with the number of pots won or lost because they'll always be different sizes, and one win therefore does not always equal another win.

This chapter may be short, but it's very important. Overcalling correctly is essential, because you have a chance to do the wrong thing so many times during the course of a game. When you have an opportunity to put a lot of big bets per hour into action, you can see that an incorrect strategy can have an immediate, huge, and negative impact on your hourly rate. This aspect of the game is one that you can work on easily, and the effort is certainly worth your time. Good luck.

DOMINATED HANDS

The term **dominated hand** refers to your two hole cards. It simply means a hand that's inferior to another hand before the flop. There are five ways that a hand can be dominated:

1. Two players (unknowingly, of course) share a common card, and one has a higher side card than the other. The most clear and common example of this situation is when one player has AK, and another player also has an ace, but his second card is lower than a king. Here the AK dominates the other hand. No matter what the other player's second card is, he's almost always a 3-1 underdog to the first player.

2. One player holds a pocket pair, and another player holds a higher pocket pair. In this situation, the higher pocket pair is about a 4-1 favorite over the lower pair. 22 is a dominated hand if any other player in the game holds a pocket pair.

3. Both of a player's cards are lower than both of another player's cards. If you hold KJ, and your opponent holds 98, then your hand dominates his.

4. A player has a hand with flush potential, but another player holds higher flush cards of the same suit. A♠ 5♠ dominates Q♠ J♠, because it makes a higher flush. If the A♠ 5♠ happens to be A♠ K♠ instead, then the Q♠ J♠ is dominated in two different ways. It can't beat the ace-high flush, and it also can't beat the A♠ K♠.

5. A player has two unpaired cards, and another player holds a pocket pair. In the most extreme example, AK is a 6.1% underdog to 22.

The following pages contain a series of tables that will give you the raw data regarding dominated hands. I generated these tables with the help of a computer. Each hand was played 500,000 times to ensure that the results were accurate to within 99.99%. That's within one hand for every ten thousand hands played.

Each hand was played to the river, with neither player folding. These tables should give you an idea of each hand's relative strength without your having to factor in different styles of play. All numbers in these tables are percentages, and the ODDS-1 column refers to the odds against the losing hand.

Table 1: AK vs. AX

AK	AQ	TIE	ODDS-1
71.76	23.65	4.59	2.85
AK	AJ		
71.46	23.98	4.57	2.81
AK	A10		
71.10	24.34	4.56	2.76
AK	A9		
71.50	23.85	4.65	2.82
AK	A8		
71.31	24.06	4.64	2.79
AK	A7		
70.84	24.50	4.66	2.73
AK	A6		
71.48	24.24	4.28	2.79
AK	A5		
69.90	25.40	4.70	2.60
AK	A4		
70.71	24.44	4.85	2.72
AK	A3		
70.66	24.50	4.52	2.71
AK	A2		
71.37	23.71	4.52	2.82

Table 1 tells you how you'll do with AK against a single opponent with an ace, when you both play to the river. If you have position on your opponent, your chances are actually even higher, since your opponent will often fold before the river if he doesn't flop anything.

Table 2: PAIR vs. PAIR

		TIE	ODDS-1
AA	KK		
81.00	18.62	0.38	4.32
AA	QQ		
80.68	18.96	0.35	4.23
AA	JJ		
80.27	19.40	0.32	4.11
AA	1010		
79.95	19.75	0.30	4.02
AA	99		
80.04	19.67	0.29	4.05
AA	88		
79.66	20.09	0.29	3.95
AA	77		
79.55	20.18	0.27	3.92
AA	66		
79.50	20.22	0.28	3.91
AA	55		
80.02	19.63	0.35	4.05
AA	44		
80.44	19.16	0.39	4.17
AA	33		
80.84	18.72	0.44	4.28
AA	22		
81.41	18.10	0.49	4.45
KK	QQ		
81.05	18.57	0.38	4.33

DOMINATED HANDS

KK	JJ	TIE	ODDS-1
80.61	19.03	0.35	4.21
KK	1010		
80.29	19.38	0.33	4.12
KK	99		
80.06	19.63	0.31	4.05
KK	88		
80.03	19.67	0.31	4.05
KK	77		
79.66	20.02	0.27	3.95
KK	66		
79.65	20.08	0.27	3.95
KK	55		
79.64	20.02	0.34	3.95
KK	44		
80.06	19.56	0.38	4.06
KK	33		
80.40	19.16	0.44	4.16
KK	22		
80.93	18.57	0.50	4.31
QQ	JJ		
81.09	18.54	0.38	4.34
QQ	1010		
80.74	18.93	0.33	4.24
QQ	99		
80.44	19.25	0.31	4.15
QQ	88		
80.07	19.63	0.30	4.06

QQ	77	TIE	ODDS-1
80.08	19.64	0.28	4.06
QQ	66		
79.57	20.15	0.28	3.93
QQ	55		
79.67	20.01	0.32	3.96
QQ	44		
80.20	19.44	0.36	4.10
QQ	33		
80.54	19.04	0.42	4.18
QQ	22		
80.96	18.56	0.34	4.32
JJ	1010		
81.10	18.55	0.34	4.34
JJ	99		
80.85	18.81	0.35	4.27
JJ	88		
80.37	19.29	0.34	4.14
JJ	77		
80.05	19.64	0.32	4.05
JJ	66		
80.15	19.54	0.31	4.08
JJ	55		
79.84	19.54	0.31	4.00
JJ	44		
80.09	19.54	0.37	4.07
JJ	33		
80.62	18.54	0.45	4.22

DOMINATED HANDS

JJ	22	TIE	ODDS-1
80.92	18.58	0.51	4.31
1010	99		
81.07	18.51	0.42	4.34
1010	88		
80.75	18.85	0.39	4.25
1010	77		
80.34	19.26	0.40	4.14
1010	66		
80.03	19.58	0.39	4.06
1010	55		
80.16	19.41	0.42	4.10
1010	44		
80.13	19.41	0.45	4.09
1010	33		
80.46	19.04	0.50	4.18
1010	22		
80.88	18.55	.57	4.31
99	88		
80.89	18.53	0.59	4.31
99	77		
80.61	18.79	0.60	4.24
99	66		
80.22	19.21	0.57	4.13
99	55		
79.89	19.50	0.60	4.05
99	44		
80.33	19.01	0.66	4.20

99	33	TIE	ODDS-1
80.43	198.92	0.65	4.20
99	22		
80.71	18.54	0.76	4.29
88	77		
80.78	18.33	0.89	4.33
88	66		
80.35	18.81	0.84	4.20
88	55		
79.92	19.17	0.91	4.10
88	44		
79.96	19.11	0.93	4.11
88	33		
80.43	18.61	0.96	4.24
88	22		
80.50	18.51	0.99	4.26
77	66		
80.24	18.48	1.28	4.23
77	55		
79.96	18.73	1.31	4.16
77	44		
79.94	18.74	1.31	4.15
77	33		
80.09	18.53	1.38	4.20
77	22		
80.42	18.16	1.43	4.30
66	55		
79.65	18.49	1.86	4.15

DOMINATED HANDS

66	44	TIE	ODDS-1
79.63	18.46	1.91	4.15
66	**33**		
79.78	18.29	1.94	4.19
66	**22**		
79.85	18.12	2.03	4.23
55	**44**		
79.55	17.81	2.64	4.23
55	**33**		
79.44	17.88	2.86	4.20
55	**22**		
79.52	17.71	2.76	4.24
44	**33**		
78.46	17.86	3.69	4.08
44	**22**		
78.50	17.97	3.71	4.09
33	**22**		
77.28	17.76	4.96	3.94

You don't have to memorize these numbers. Here's the main idea I want you to take from Table 2:

If you have a pocket pair and another player has a pocket pair higher than yours, you have only about a 20% chance of winning the hand, *regardless of what your pair is.*

Let's say you hold 2♠ 2♥ and the player on your right raises. Then he genuinely accidentally exposes his cards just enough for you to see that he's holding A♠ A♣. You would probably fold your deuces.

But what if you were holding K♦ K♠ instead of those deuces? Would you fold then? If not, then why? What's the difference? As you can see from the table, if the other player has a pocket pair higher than yours, it doesn't matter what your pair is. Pocket kings are only one-half of one percent better than pocket deuces.

In other words, with *any* pocket pair, if someone else's is higher than yours, you are a 4-1 underdog.

Table 3: AK vs. PAIR

AA	AK	TIE	ODDS-1
92.02	6.74	1.24	13.84

KK	AK		
69.55	29.66	0.79	2.33

QQ	AK		
56.96	42.71	0.33	1.33

JJ	AK		
57.10	42.58	0.32	1.34

1010	AK		
57.12	42.57	0.31	1.34

99	AK		
55.35	44.33	0.32	1.25

88	AK		
55.44	44.27	0.29	1.25

77	AK		
55.15	44.56	0.28	1.24

66	AK		
55.24	44.45	0.31	1.24

55	AK		
54.77	44.85	0.38	1.22

44	AK		
54.28	45.27	0.44	1.20

33	AK		
53.48	46.01	0.51	1.16

22	AK		
52.75	46.67	0.58	1.13

Whenever there are only two players to see the flop (and especially if one or both of them raised before it), the most common type of matchup you'll see is that one player will have AK and the other will have a pocket pair. Table 3 shows how these compare.

If you hold AK, the worst case scenario is when your opponent holds AA or KK. Even when your opponent holds pocket queens or below, though, your chances of winning are between 42% and 46%—not very good odds in a head-up game.

Table 4: AXS vs. 1 RANDOM HAND (1RH)

AKs	1RH	TIE	ODDS-1
66.22	32.12	1.66	2.04
AQs	1RH		
65.20	33.01	1.79	1.95
AJs	1RH		
64.41	33.64	1.95	1.89
A10s	1RH		
63.38	34.38	2.24	1.82
A9s	1RH		
61.44	36-04	2.53	1.68
A8s	1RH		
60.54	36.60	2.87	1.63
A7s	1RH		
59.39	37.43	3.18	1.56
A6s	1RH		
58.39	38.17	3.44	1.51
A5s	1RH		
58.07	38.20	3.73	1.50
A4s	1RH		
57.11	39.07	3.82	1.44
A3s	1RH		
57.36	39.92	3.72	1.39
A2s	1RH		
55.52	40.71	3.77	1.35

If you read the chapter on raising and have been following my advice about how to play in late position, you will often be in a situation where you've raised in late position with AX suited and you have just one opponent (usually the big blind) to see the flop with you. Table 4 shows you how you will do against that one player.

As you can see, when you have no information at all about your opponent's hand, you'll win anywhere from 55% to 66% of the time. Remember, however, that if he did call a raise before the flop, his hand is probably better than a random, average hand and your winning percentages won't be as high at 66%.

Table 5: PAIR vs. 1 RH

AA	1RH	TIE	ODDS-1
84.96	14.51	0.53	5.77
KK	**1RH**		
82.13	17.30	0.56	4.69
QQ	**1RH**		
79.65	19.77	0.58	3.99
JJ	**1RH**		
77.10	22.26	0.64	3.43
1010	**1RH**		
74.70	24.63	0.67	3.01
99	**1RH**		
71.65	27.55	0.80	2.58
88	**1RH**		
68.78	30.34	0.89	2.25
77	**1RH**		
65.74	33.23	1.03	1.96
66	**1RH**		
62.64	36.22	1.15	1.72
55	**1RH**		
59.60	39.06	1.34	1.52
44	**1RH**		
56.34	42.12	1.54	1.33
33	**1RH**		
52.90	45.39	1.71	1.16
22	**1RH**		
49.40	48.70	1.90	1.01

(Here and in all other charts, "RH" stands for "Random Hand")

You'll be a favorite over any random hand if you hold a pocket pair. Remember, though, that your opponent's hand is probably better than random if he called a raise before the flop with it. Consider that when evaluating your chances.

Notice, however, that a pair of deuces is only even money against a random hand, while it is a 6% favorite against AK. How can that be? It's because some of the random hands that figure in the overall statistics will be pocket pairs higher than deuces.

Table 6: TOP 5 CARDS vs. 1 RH			
AK	1RH	TIE	ODDS-1
64.33	33.95	1.72	1.87
AQ	1RH		
63.69	34.49	1.82	1.82
AJ	1RH		
62.52	35.44	2.04	1.74
A10	1RH		
61.73	35.96	2.31	1.69
KQ	1RH		
60.38	37.56	2.06	1.59
KJ	1RH		
59.45	38.96	1.25	1.54
K10	1RH		
58.56	38.96	2.25	1.49
QJ	1RH		
56.91	40.67	2.42	1.39
Q10	1RH		
55.98	41.36	2.66	1.34
J10	1RH		
53.82	43.31	2.87	1.23

Almost everyone plays to see the flop when they hold two of the top five cards (ace, king, queen, jack and 10). These five cards can combine to make ten different hands: AK, AQ, AJ, A10, KQ, KJ, K10, QJ, Q10 and J10. Unless you hold two of the lower cards (Q, jack or 10) in early position, these are usually very good cards. They add up to 20 or 21, and they should show a profit in the long run if played properly.

Remember, some of the random hands will be pocket pairs or two cards higher than yours. If you hold J10, someone else will already have you beat before the flop 50% of the time. If your cards are suited, you can add 3% to your winning percentages and subtract 3% from the opponent's winning percentages, thereby improving your chances by 6%.

Table 7: GROUP 1 HANDS vs. 1 RH

	1RH	TIE	ODDS-1
AA 84.96	14.51	0.53	5.78
KK 82.13	17.30	0.56	4.69
QQ 79.65	19.77	0.58	3.99
JJ 77.10	22.26	0.64	3.43
AKs 66.22	32.12	1.66	2.04

Table 8: GROUP 2 HANDS vs. 1 RH

1010	1RH	TIE	ODDS-1
74.70	24.63	0.67	3.01
AQs	1RH		
65.20	33.01	1.79	1.95
AJs	1RH		
64.41	33.64	1.95	1.89
KQs	1RH		
62.37	35.64	1.99	1.73
AK	1RH		
64.33	33.95	1.72	1.87

Table 9: GROUP 3 HANDS vs. 1 RH

99	1RH	TIE	ODDS-1
71.65	27.55	0.80	2.58
AQ	1RH		
63.69	34.49	1.82	1.82
A10s	1RH		
63.38	34.38	2.24	1.82
KJs	1RH		
61.46	36.33	2.20	1.67
QJs	1RH		
59.10	38.51	2.39	1.52
J10s	1RH		
56.19	41.05	2.75	1.36

Structure Your Learning
Assignment #18

The main purpose of this chapter is to make you realize that some hands are very big underdogs to other hands, especially when played head-up before the flop. There will be many times during the course of your playing career when a player will raise before the flop and you'll be the only player left to call that raise. Often you will be in the big blind. Most of the time your best play will be to fold your cards and go on to the next hand. These tables should help you see why.

You do not have to memorize these statistics. All I want is for you to get a general idea of how bad the odds are against a hand that is dominated before the flop. Be aware that the concept of dominated hands exists, and it's very costly not to know about them. Your assignment is to complete the following open book test. Answers follow the questions. Good luck.

1. If you hold AK, your sole opponent holds an ace with another random card, and you both play to the river, you will win the hand about _____% of the time.

2. If you hold a pocket pair, your sole opponent holds a lower pocket pair, and you both play to the river, you will win the hand about _____% of the time.

3. If you hold AK, your sole opponent holds a pocket pair of queens or below, and you both play to the river, you will win the hand about _____% of the time.

4. If you hold AXs, your sole opponent holds a random hand, and you both play to the river, you will win the hand about _____% of the time.

5. What's the most important thing to keep in mind when your opponent has a random hand and called your raise before the flop?

6. If you hold a pocket pair, your sole opponent holds a random hand, and you both play to the river, you will win the hand about _____% of the time.

7. If you hold two of the top five cards, your sole opponents holds a random hand, and you both play to the river, you will win the hand about _____% of the time.

8. If you hold a Group 1 hand, your sole opponent holds a random hand, and you both play to the river, you will win the hand about _____% of the time.

9. If you hold a Group 2 hand, your sole opponent holds a random hand, and you both play to the river, you will win the hand about _____% of the time.

10. If you hold a Group 3 hand, your sole opponent holds a random hand, and you both play to the river, you will win the hand about _____% of the time.

Answers to Assignment #18

1. 70-71

2. 79-81

3. 42-46

4. 55-66

5. Some of your opponents' random hands will be a pocket pair higher than yours or two cards higher than yours, and then it will be your hand that's dominated.

6. 59-85

7. 53-64

8. 66-85

9. 64-75

10. 56-72

PLAYING ON THE FLOP

The flop is the defining moment in the hand. After the flop, your hand will usually go one of two ways:

1. You'll miss what you were hoping for and fold.

2. You'll flop a great hand (or a good straight or flush draw) and play to the river.

To play past the flop, you should have flopped:

1. The best hand.
2. A draw to the best hand.
3. The probable best hand.
4. A draw to the probable best hand.

This rule describes two entirely different types of hands. For example, if you have A♥ K♥, and the flop is Q♠ J♣ 10♦, Q♥ 8♥ 3♥, or A♠ A♣ K♠, then you've flopped the nuts. If the flop is J♠ 10♣ 5♥ or 9♥ 7♥ 4♦, then you've flopped a draw to the best hand.

It's parts 3 and 4 of the rule that cause differences of opinion. You see various amounts and patterns of betting and raising specifically because players have different interpretations of those parts of the rule. Everybody has their own idea of what constitutes the probable best hand or a draw to the probable best hand. I'll try to help you answer this question for yourself by showing you some common situations.

We're not going to waste our time studying how to play hands like J♥ 5♣ or 8♠ 3♦, because the only time you'll see the flop with these hands is when you're in the big blind and no one has raised to make you fold. Hopefully, your good poker sense will tell you how to play these hands when you see them.

Instead, I've chosen ten hands that you should usually see the flop with: A♦ A♠, Q♣ Q♠, A♣ K♣, A♣ K♦, 10♠ 10♥, A♠ J♠, 9♣ 9♥, A♦ 10♦, Q♣ J♠, and J♠ 10♥. We'll look at how they each fare with three different flops.

I. The flop is A♥ J♣ 5♠.

1. A♦ A♠ - You've flopped a set of aces. Beware of a king, queen, or 10 that would make someone a straight. You should also watch out for the (less likely but possible) 2, 3, or 4, to make someone a wheel.

2. Q♣ Q♠ - The ace overcard is the worst one you could get. If there's a bet, you have to fold.

3. A♣ K♣ - You have top pair with top kicker. This hand plays best against a small field and against another player with an ace. There's even another club on the flop, giving you a backdoor flush draw.

4. A♣ K♦ - Again, top pair with top kicker.

5. 10♠ 10♥ - Two overcards. It's too much to hope no one holds an ace or a jack, especially against a large field.

6. A♠ J♠ - Top two pair. You must raise to protect this hand, because any time two of the top five cards come on the flop, there's a possible straight draw. You should consider check-raising if it will help knock players out. You also have the added potential of a backdoor flush.

7. 9♣ 9♥ - You should probably fold. You had to flop another 9 or something like 6♥ 7♣ 8♠ to have a good hand. A flop like 7♠ 8♣ 10♦ would also have helped, since your hand takes an extra 9 out of the deck. In that case, if you made your open-end straight, you'd be less likely to have to split the pot, because you hold two 9s.

8. A♦ 10♦ - A pair of aces with a 10 kicker. Your main worry is if your opponent has a higher kicker.

9. Q♣ J♠ - You have a pair of jacks and no flush draw. You're hoping you don't have to call a bet.

10. J♠ 10♥ - You have a pair of jacks and sort of a straight draw. You don't have the best hand at this point, so you should probably fold if there's a bet.

II. The flop is K♠ 10♣ 8♦.

1. A♦ A♠ - You probably have the best hand, except for that occasional time when someone holds a king and a 10, which is all too common in low limit games.

2. Q♣ Q♠ - The king overcard is not that bad—at least it's not an ace. I might bet if I'm first and there are just one or two players. If someone bets into you here, you just have to decide for yourself if the bettor has a king.

3. A♣ K♣ - You have top pair with top kicker and a backdoor flush draw. Watch out for the straight draw.

4. A♣ K♦ - Same as above, except there's no flush draw.

5. 10♠ 10♥ - You've flopped a set of 10s, but look out for the possible straight draw.

6. A♠ J♠ - You have a gutshot straight draw and a backdoor flush draw. Getting another ace will sometimes give you a winning hand.

7. 9♣ 9♥ - You needed another 9, and the two overcards kill your hand. Fold if there's a bet.

8. A♦ 10♦ - You have middle pair with top kicker, which is sometimes a good hand; another player does not always have one of the top cards on the flop. You also have a backdoor flush draw.

9. Q♣ J♠ - You have an open-end straight, which should win a big pot if you get a 9 or an ace.

10. J♠ 10♥ - You have a pair of 10s with a jack kicker, not a good hand against a lot of players. And no, three cards to a straight is not a straight draw.

III. The flop is Q♦ 9♦ 7♣.

1. A♦ A♠ - You have the probable best hand, but you have to watch out for the straight draws (anyone holding 56, 58, 68, 610, 810, 8J, 10J, 10K, or JK has a straight draw). Your hand is very vulnerable. You also have a backdoor flush draw.

2. Q♣ Q♠ - You have a set of queens, but watch out for the straight and flush draws. You almost need a full house to win this hand against a lot of players.

3. A♣ K♣ - You've missed the flop, so you should usually let it go if there's a bet and a lot of opposition. You have a backdoor flush draw, but it's not worth pursuing unless the turn card is also a straight card for you, such as the J♣ or 10♣.

4. A♣ K♦ - Same as above, plus the added benefit of a draw to a straight flush.

5. 10♠ 10♥ - All those straight draws and the possible flush draws, coupled with the overcard, make your hand unplayable. You're really hoping for a check.

6. A♠ J♠ - You missed the flop and don't have any kind of draw. Many players make the mistake of calling, hoping to catch an ace. Don't do it.

7. 9♣ 9♥ - You have a set of 9s and the probable best hand at this point. Any diamond and any card between a 5 and a king (except a card that pairs the board) could kill your hand.

8. A♦ 10♦ - You have the nut flush draw, and the right turn card could also give you a straight draw. This is a good hand that you might raise with in late position.

9. Q♣ J♠ - You have a pair of queens with a jack kicker. If there was no raise before the flop, you'll often have the best hand at this point against a small field. A preflop raise means you have a dominated hand even though you made a pair with it.

10. J♠ 10♥ - You have an open end straight draw, but you have to beware of the flush draw.

Here's a short list of points to keep in mind when playing on the flop:

PLAYING ON THE FLOP

1. If you hold AK and you flop another ace or king, giving you top pair with top kicker, you should occasionally check-raise on the flop. Varying your play in this way will make your hand a little less easy to read.

2. If you hold two big cards and the flop is three small cards, you should usually check and fold if there's a bet and a lot of opponents. If there's just one player to take a shot at you, then you have to consider everything you know about your opponent. Sometimes, A♣ Q♥ is still the best hand, even when the flop is 8♥ 5♦ 2♣.

3. The flop is a key point in the play of the hand. Resist the temptation to call when you actually have a hand you should fold. Mistakes made after the flop are twice as expensive as mistakes made before it.

4. If you're about to call a bet on the flop, ask yourself why folding or raising is not a better option. By now you know five good reasons to raise. You also know when you're likely to be holding a dominated hand.

5. If you're truly undecided about how to play your hand when you see the flop, you should usually fold if the pot is very small, and you should usually call if the pot is very large. Remember, this advice applies only to those times when you really don't know what to do.

6. If you happen to be short-stacked, or there's a chance you'll go all-in during this hand, keep in mind that the most important thing is to win the hand. Don't be concerned about the size of the pot, the pot odds, deception or anything else. Do whatever it takes to win the hand, even if you have to play it in an unconventional manner.

7. If you raised before the flop and totally missed on it, resist the urge to continue if you have to play against a large field. Learn to check and fold (even with big cards), when it's the right thing to do.

8. If you are check-raised on the flop, you should usually give up all but the best of hands. Don't be embarrassed to bet and then throw the hand away when a player check-raises. You don't have to call to save face. If you fold, and it turns out that you made the right move, other players will secretly admire you. Besides, what do you think the check-raise means?

9. If a lot of players see the flop, and no one raised before it, then someone will often flop a set. If eight players see the flop, and it comes 8♣ 6♥ 4♦, don't be surprised if someone shows pocket 6s at the end of the hand.

PLAYING ON THE FLOP

Flopping a Completed Hand

To flop a completed hand means to flop a straight or above. Here are the five kinds of completed hands:

1. Straight
2. Flush
3. Full House
4. Four of a kind
5. Straight-flush

How you play when you flop a completed hand depends mainly on two things:

1. The vulnerability of your hand.
2. The number of opponents you're facing.

Let's look at each type of hand in light of these two factors:

1. *Straight*. If you hold A♦ K♥, and the flop is Q♣ J♠ 10♦, you don't have to worry about a higher straight draw, and the odds against a single player making a backdoor flush on you are about 22-1. Against one player, you're a big favorite to win the hand.

If you hold 9♠ 8♣, and the flop is that same Q♣ J♠ 10♦, you still have a straight, but anyone holding an ace or a king will beat you if another ace or king comes. If there are six or seven other players in the hand, someone could likely have two pair or trips. If the board pairs on the turn or river, you could be in trouble.

If the flop is Q♦ J♥ 10♦, and there are six players, then another diamond might make someone else a flush. Against only one opponent that's not so likely.

2. *Flush.* If you hold K♣ 9♣, and the flop is J♣ 7♣ 2♣, you have a good hand. If there are a lot of players, though, and another club comes, someone holding the A♣ has just beaten you. If the board pairs, someone could hold a full house. Against just one player, though, a scare card is likely to be just that, not a real threat.

3. *Full House.* A full house is usually a great hand in poker. In hold'em, though, everything is situational and must be considered in light of the flop. If you hold 2♥ 2♦, and the flop is 2♣ A♣ A♠, you have a very vulnerable hand.

Anyone holding another ace could hit his kicker on the turn or river to make a higher full house. You'll probably win this hand against just one player, but you may lose against a lot of players. You even have to worry about a player holding pocket 3s getting another 3 on the turn or river.

4. *Four of a kind.* Finally, we're looking at a hand you don't have to worry about. If you hold 6♣ 6♥, and the flop is 9♦ 6♦ 6♠, your hand is insured. Do you know why? Take a second and see if you can figure it out.

It's because if you lose with this hand, you'll win the hold'em jackpot. You actually want everyone at the table in on this one. If the jackpot is bigger than a few hundred dollars, you're even hoping to get beat.

5. *Straight flush.* Just like with the four of a kind, you'd like to lose with this hand. About a month ago I was in a hold'em game with, as luck would have it, eight players who had reputations for being good, solid, no-nonsense, high-card players. They all called, telling me that a lot of high cards were gone from the deck. I was on the button, and when I looked at my hand I saw that I held the 3♣ 2♣. I raised! Not because I had great cards, but because I wanted to vary my play, misrepresent my hand, and win a bigger pot if I won the hand. I was totally prepared, both emotionally and physically, to throw it away on the flop if I missed. It was reraised and I capped it!

I got the flop of a lifetime. It was 4♣ 5♣ 6♣— a straight flush! I hope right now you're thinking what I was when I saw the flop: "I hope I lose this hand." I was praying that someone held the 7♣ or the 8♣ and that the other one would come on the turn or river. It didn't happen, but I did win the hand and a nice pot. Everyone who could beat pocket kings or aces (since that's what I represented) called me all the way to the river.

Special Flops

There are two types of flops that deserve special mention: when the flop is all of one suit, and when the flop contains a pair. These two kinds of flops require a little extra skill to play.

When the flop is all of the same suit:
1. Don't allow your opponents to have any free cards if you flopped a flush. This is particularly important if you have a small flush, and anyone holding a flush card could beat you if a fourth flush card comes on the turn or river.

2. If you flop the nut flush, you'll probably win the hand. You might want to check on the flop to give the impression that you're drawing to a flush like everyone else. You can bet (or even check-raise) on the turn.

3. Don't forget about tells. Players who double-check their hands immediately upon seeing the flop usually have exactly one card of that suit.

4. Don't draw to a flush if it's not ace- or king-high. It's just too expensive considering the fact that you'll make the flush only one-third of the time, and you might lose when you do make it. If you have an opponent in this situation, he must have something.

When the flop contains a pair:
1. Consider how big the pair is. The higher the pair, the more likely it is that someone has flopped three of a kind. If it's a baby pair, and especially if there aren't many players in the hand, it's likely that no one has one of those cards to make three of a kind (they wouldn't have stayed in to see the flop if they did).

2. Look at the other card that came on the flop with the pair. Does it make two cards of the same suit or a possible straight draw? If all three cards are 9 or higher, there's probably a straight draw.

3. If you have a pocket pair that's higher than the pair on the flop, you should play your hand carefully. You can win by having the best hand (two pair). If someone does have the trips, you can also win by getting one of your hole cards on the turn or river.

4. If you have the trips, your kicker is very important. If you get any serious action, the other player could also have trips. If you think he does, it's really just a contest of kickers.

5. If the pair on the flop is low and you don't think it hit anyone, you can bluff at the pot. I recommend that you check on the flop and then bet it out on the turn. This keeps the pot small and makes it easier for your opponent to fold on the turn.

Structure Your Learning
Assignment #19
Recall the rule for playing past the flop, especially the part about the best probable hand or a draw to the best probable hand. Next time you play in your usual game, keep track of those times you flop what you think is the best probable hand or a draw to the best probable hand. If you lose those hands, I want you to evaluate your play and decide why you lost.

There are many reasons you can lose a hand. You might never have had the best hand on the flop to begin with. Maybe you had a pair and your opponent made his very reasonable draw to a straight or a flush. He could also have made a very unreasonable draw to a straight or a flush.

You could have lost to a backdoor flush-draw (i.e. a very lucky opponent). Maybe you were bluffed out of the hand. Did you have a draw that just didn't get there? You could knowingly have played a bad hand before the flop. Whatever the reasons are, identify them and write them down. If you like, make a short list of reasons for losing and take it with you to each game. Each time you lose a hand, make a mark next to the appropriate reason.

After the playing session, review your notes. See if you can detect a pattern. Do you lose for one reason more than any other? Is that reason within your control? Chances are, it is. If you play as I've recommended thus far, you'll always be in a position to win the hand, and you shouldn't suffer too many bad beats. If you can eliminate some of your losses by identifying the reasons you lose, you should do so. Repeat this exercise in about a year and see if your losses are less often your own fault. Good luck.

PLAYING AGAINST THE BLINDS

When you're in a hand, you should think of everyone else in the hand as being in one of two categories:

1. In the blind
2. Not in the blind

There's a very important reason for this distinction. It's because you have two types of players in the hand, and they hold two entirely different types of hands. Generally, the players in the blinds have hands they would not otherwise enter the pot with. Players who voluntarily call the big blind and see the flop are telling you something about their hands: regardless of what you might think of their two cards, they think it's a hand worth a call.

Since they put their money in the pot before getting their cards, the blinds have totally random hands. If no one raises before the flop, you know nothing else about the big blind's hand. Since the small blind has to call a partial bet to stay in, he does give away some information when he decides to play the hand. If you're up against a player who usually folds when he's in the small blind, then if he just calls for the other portion of the blind, you may have learned something about his hand.

Sometimes, one of the players in the blinds will exercise his option to raise himself before the flop. Usually, he'll do that because he has an obviously great hand, such as AA or KK. He might just be particularly fond of his hand for other reasons.

I recommend that you never exercise the option of raising yourself when in the blinds, because I don't think the benefit of building the pot outweighs the many disadvantages:

1. You give away the fact that you have good cards early in the hand, which makes your opponents play more carefully against you from the beginning.

2. The extra small bet you got everyone to call before the flop might be less than what you could win if you had waited until the turn to raise or check-raise.

3. You're in terrible position (early) throughout the play of the entire hand.

4. If you miss your hand, you've put yourself in the position of possibly having to bluff from an early position at the end of the hand.

PLAYING AGAINST THE BLINDS

5. A raise from one of the blinds tends to build the pot rather than make players fold. A player who has called a bet and has to call only one more bet–because the blind raised–will almost always call to see the flop.

A possible exception to my rule against raising from the blind position is when you have a big pair in the pocket and there are just one, two or maybe three other players in the hand. If you go back and look at the above list of disadvantages to raising before the flop, you'll see that they're lessened with fewer players in the hand. Let your knowledge of your opponents and your understanding of the game be your guide.

Even though I advise against raising from the blinds before the flop, I do recommend that you always reraise if someone has raised before the flop and your hand warrants it. I would not raise from the big blind before the flop with KK, QQ, or AK. If someone else raised first, however, I'd certainly go ahead and reraise.

The problem with playing against a player in the blind is that you don't have all the usual tools available to help you read his hand. You can't make anything of his hand based on position, because he didn't select his hand according to his position. He got it at random. You can't resort to psychology to help read the hand, because he didn't have any say about choosing the hand. You also can't rely on statistics to figure out what the hand is, because it could be anything, since he's in the blind.

The three best tools you have to help read hands (position, psychology and statistics) are all useless when playing against the blinds early in the hand. The player in the blind literally has a secret weapon to use against you, especially if he's in the big blind, no one raised before the flop, and he did not exercise the option of raising himself.

So, how do you play against the blinds? First, be aware of a few basic facts. About four-fifths of the 1,326 possible hands are hands that most players would not voluntarily play. That means that the blind will have less than a premium hand about 80% of the time. If the flop is something like A♠ Q♥ 10♥, it's likely that the blind does not have two good cards that will fit in well with this flop. He'll probably fold if you bet.

If the flop is 9♦ 6♥ 3♣, and the big blind bets out, you can be sure the flop hit his hand, even though he has to be holding bad cards for that to happen. If he bets into a large field, if he check-raises on the flop, or if he reraises on the flop, you can be sure he has a good hand.

You can rapidly make up for the blind's advantage by being especially attentive to how he plays from the flop on. You *can* use psychology and position to help read the blind's hand, but only after the flop.

If you're in a hand against several other players and one of them is the blind, you should be aware of the fact that all bets and raises are not created equal. A bet or a raise from the blind means something entirely different than it does when coming from one of the other players. A check-raise from the blind, especially on the flop, is an excellent clue about the strength of his hand.

A player in the blind who flops a strong hand will usually not be able just to bet, knock players out, and win the hand. Why? Well, the strength of his hand is situational and temporary. A blind who holds 8♣ 3♥ when the flop is 8♥ 5♥ 3♠ will almost always have the best hand at that point. The problem for him is that there are more cards to come.

If this blind bets, he knows that the players who have overcards, a pair, a flush, or a straight draw will call, hoping to see one more card to make their hand. So he will check-raise on the flop in an attempt to knock these players out of the hand. It's a good move, and it often works. It also gives away his hand to the players astute enough to know that a check-raise from the blind usually means just what I've described.

Another reason that this blind cannot bet and win is that the draws will often have the right odds to call and possibly beat him. If he bets on the flop and gets called, it's now mathematically correct for his opponents to call again when he bets on the turn. Anyone with a draw will then have the right odds to see the final card and possibly make his hand. The check-raise is an effort to keep this very predictable scenario from happening. It's an attempt to drive players out of the hand by forcing them to call two bets cold.

A more common situation is when the flop comes and the big blind bets it out first. You're now in a difficult position as a caller, because you don't know why he's betting. Is he betting for value with a good hand, or is he taking a shot at bluffing and stealing the pot? Is he semi-bluffing with a weak, but improvable hand? Are you known as a high-card player, and he's giving you a chance to throw away your K♣ Q♦ when the flop is 6♥ 6♣ 3♠? You just have to know your players.

My experience has been that the blinds usually do not attempt to bluff on the flop. If they bet first, it's because they have a hand with which they expect to win. You have to keep in mind that what it takes to win the hand depends largely on the flop. If the flop is all low cards, and the blind bets into a large field, he's not bluffing. He expects to win the hand. If the flop is weird-looking, like J♠ 6♣ 2♦, and the blind bets into you, it's because he usually expects to win the hand.

Over the years, I've developed a strategy for playing against the blinds that has, for me, yielded superior results. It's easy to understand and easy to remember, and you shouldn't have any trouble making it part of your hold'em strategy also. Here's my rule for playing against the blinds: *throw away slightly better than average hands if the blind bets into you on the flop.*

PLAYING AGAINST THE BLINDS

Of course, what constitutes an average hand depends on the flop, your cards, your position, how many other players are in the hand, and your estimation of what the preflop action means.

There are several good reasons why this is a profitable strategy for you:

1. You're not going to win every hand after the flop anyway. You'll win only a fraction of the hands you play past the flop, and you will often have to get lucky to win some of those.

2. You have only one bet invested in the hand. It's not that expensive to let it go and wait for a hand where you can be the bettor, and not the caller.

3. You never really know what the blind has, so why play a guessing game? That's not the way to play poker.

4. You'll be calling the blind's bet fewer times than average, and when you do call, the blind will notice it. He will (correctly) put you on a very good hand. Because of that, he'll often check to you on the turn when you call on the flop, thus increasing your chances of winning the hand.

5. You will always have position on the blind, which means that you'll often be able to raise on the turn or river, thereby getting in an extra big bet from the losing hands. This benefit more than makes up for the times when you folded on the flop and forfeited a small bet with an average hand.

Learn to slow down when you have a big overpair and you're playing against the blinds. If you have Q♥ Q♣ and the flop is J♠ 7♣ 5♥, your hand may be good, but it's not great if the blind bets into you. Except for another queen, there's almost no card in the deck that I like on the turn or river.

A 5♦ or 5♠ gives you two pair, but what if he's holding J♣ 5♣ or A♠ 5♣? How do you know that an ace or a king on the turn doesn't beat you? Even a harmless looking deuce could make him two pair. Remember, he's in the blind, so he could have anything.

So what do you do? You should usually just call with an overpair if the blind bets into you and there's just the two of you in the hand. If there are other players in the hand, then you will sometimes want to raise to thin the field, which will increase your chances of winning the hand.

As a reminder, don't forget that the entire nature of Texas hold'em (and any other poker game) is that it's a game of concealed information. When the flop is K♣ 7♥ 4♦ and the big blind bets into you, you can think to yourself, "I'm going to fold my K♠ 8♠, because he's in the blind, and his kicker could be better than mine. Or he might have two pair, and I just don't want to play a guessing game and pay him off all the way to the river, never knowing for sure where I stand."

You can think all that, just don't say it out loud. The idea of playing differently against the blinds is a little-known concept among lower limit players, so you should want to be the one player in your game to take advantage of it.

Structure Your Learning
Assignment #20
Next time you play in your usual hold'em game, I want you to keep track of every time you fold a hand on the flop when playing against the blind. We're interested only in those times when you would have called a bet from a player not in the blind, but did not call simply because the player who bet was in the blind position. After you fold the hand, keep track of how much money you've saved yourself.

OUTS

An **out** is a card that helps improve a poker hand. If you hold 8♦ 7♦, and the flop is A♦ J♣ 3♦, there are nine diamonds, or nine "outs," that will make your hand. You should always have an idea of how many outs you have, because your number of outs determines how (or even if) you should play the hand. Here's a list of the most common hands you'll be playing, with some sample flops and the outs for each hand:

1. A♦ A♠. The flop is A♥ 9♣ 5♣.
You have seven outs to make a full house or better: A♣, 9♠, 9♥, 9♦, 5♠, 5♥, and 5♦.

2. J♦ J♠. The flop is Q♦ 9♥ 8♣.
Only four cards will make a straight: 10♠, 10♣, 10♥, and 10♦. You have just two outs to make three of a kind: J♣ and J♥. If you do make three jacks on the turn, you have ten outs to make a full house or better: Q♠, Q♣, Q♥, the other jack, 9♠, 9♣, 9♦, 8♠, 8♥, and 8♦.

3. A♦ K♦. The flop is Q♦ 10♥ 6♦.

You have twelve outs to improve. The J♠, J♣, and J♥ will make you a straight. Nine other cards will make you a flush: J♦, 10♦, 9♦, 8♦, 7♦, 5♦, 4♦, 3♦, and 2♦.

4. A♦ K♠. The flop is K♥ Q♦ 10♦.

Two cards, the K♣ and the K♦, will give you three kings. Any one of the four jacks will give you a straight. Any one of the other eight diamonds, while not improving your hand, gives you a four-flush to draw to.

5. A♦ J♠. The flop is J♦ 8♣ 5♠.

You have five outs to improve: the A♠, A♣, A♥, J♣, and the J♥. Yes, another 8 or 5 makes you two pair, but they don't count as outs because they give other players the same extra pair they give you, so you get no advantage.

6. A♦ 5♥. The flop is A♥ 9♣ 5♣.

Four cards will make a full house: the A♠, A♣, 5♠, and the 5♦.

7. K♦ Q♦. The flop is J♦ 10♦ 2♥.

The A♦ makes you a royal flush, and the 9♦ makes you a straight-flush. You have thirteen other outs to make a straight or a flush: A♠, A♣, A♥, 9♠, 9♣, 9♥, 8♦, 7♦, 6♦, 5♦, 4♦, 3♦, and the 2♦. You also have three kings and three queens to make a pair of kings or queens, which sometimes wins the hand.

8. K♦ Q♠. The flop is J♦ 10♥ 9♣.

You have...no outs. You've flopped a completed hand–a straight–and you can't improve it unless you can make a backdoor flush, which is not possible with this flop. To make a backdoor flush or straight, you must have three parts of the hand on the flop; then, of course, you have to get the other two parts on the turn and the river.

9. K♦ 10♠. The flop is 8♣ 7♠ 3♦.

You have six outs to make a pair: K♠, K♣, K♥, 10♣, 10♥, and 10♦. Any of the four 9s on the turn will give you an open-end straight draw, which adds eight more outs for the river.

10. Q♦ J♠. The flop is Q♥ 10♥ 9♣.

You have ten outs for a straight here: K♠, K♣, K♥, K♦, 8♠, 8♣, 8♥, and 8♦. The Q♠ or the Q♣ also makes you three queens.

11. Q♦ 9♠. The flop is J♣ 6♠ 3♦.

You have six outs for even a pair here: Q♠, Q♣, Q♥, 9♣, 9♥, and 9♦. Be aware of the fact that making a pair of 9s does improve your hand, but the result might not be the best hand with the J♣ overcard on the flop. A 10 on the turn may actually be more helpful, since it gives you an open-end straight to draw to, which adds eight more outs to your hand.

12. J♦ 10♦. The flop is J♠ 10♥ 8♦.

You have four outs to turn your two pair into a full house here: J♥, J♣, 10♣, and 10♠. If you instead get another diamond on the turn, you'll then have nine more outs to make a flush. If that turn card is the 9♦, you'll also have picked up eight more outs to make a straight on the river.

13. J♦ 10♠. The flop is A♦ K♥ 8♣.

You have only four outs to make the straight: Q♠, Q♣, Q♥, and Q♦.

14. 9♦ 8♦. The flop is 9♣ 7♠ 6♥.

You have thirteen outs here: 9♠ and 9♥ to make trips, 8♠, 8♣, and 8♥ to make two pair, and 10♠, 10♣, 10♥, 10♦, 5♠, 5♣, 5♥, and 5♦ to make the open-end straight draw.

These examples cover most of the common situations you'll encounter in a hold'em game. The hands you'll be holding and the flops you'll get are limited in number, so the combination of the two will produce the same situations repeatedly. Once you get into the habit of thinking about the number of outs you have, it won't take you long to be able to count outs without thinking about it.

There's another perspective to counting outs: looking at the situation from your opponents' points of view. For example, look again at the fifth situation above (where you hold A♦ J♠, and the flop is J♦ 8♣ 5♠). Assume there are six other players in the hand with you, as is often the case in a good game. Let's say that their hands are as follows:

OUTS

1. K♠ K♣ (already has you beat; two outs: K♥, K♦)

2. Q♥ 10♣ (four outs to make a straight: all four 9s).

3. 10♦ 9♥ (eight outs: all four queens and all four 7s).

4. 7♥ 6♣ (eight outs: all four 9s and all four 4s).

5. 5♥ 5♣ (six outs to make four of a kind or a full house: 5♦, 8♠, 8♥, 8♦, J♣, and J♥—remember that you hold the J♠—and any card that doesn't pair the board adds three more outs for the river).

6. 6♣ 4♥ (four outs: all four 7s).

You've flopped top pair with top kicker, a hand that you'd ordinarily think is a good hand. Yet any one of twenty-seven different cards on the turn will beat you, and there's not even a four-flush possible on the flop! Your vulnerability is determined by how many players you're facing and whether the flop is coordinated well for them.

The purpose of this chapter is to make you think about outs. Sometimes, you're going to play your hand to the end anyway, your opponents' outs be damned. Sometimes, though, your hand might be so middling that you could be persuaded to give it up early on, if you realize that you're facing so many players with so many outs. Learn to think ahead and look at the situation from your opponents' points of view. It pays.

POT ODDS

The concept of **pot odds** is easy to understand. It's simply the relationship, expressed as a ratio, between the size of the bet you are making or calling and the number of those bets in the pot. For example, if there is $12 in the pot and you have to call a $3 bet, then you are getting pot odds of 4 to 1, expressed as 4:1.

The "4" in the above equation is the number of bets in the pot (not the amount of money), and the "1" in the equation represents your bet. If you have to call $6 with that same $12 in the pot, you're getting pot odds of 2:1. If you have to call $8 with a $12 pot, you're getting pots odds of 1.5:1.

Oddsmakers sometimes factor out any fractions to make the odds easier to understand. They do so by multiplying the odds by two or three. Odds of 1.5:1 becomes odds of 3:2, and odds of 3.5:1 becomes 7:2. It's exactly the same thing; it's just easier to read and to understand.

> *Test Your Knowledge #5*
> Continuing with the above example, what
> are your pot odds if you have to call $9 with
> a $12 pot? Can you express those odds with-
> out the fraction?
> Answer at the end of the chapter.

When you have a hand you know you're going to be playing, you should always be aware of what the pot odds are. That's relatively easy to do once you know how and get into the habit. You can take my word for it now that knowing the pot odds will have a positive effect on your hourly rate.

To know your pot odds, all you have to do is count the number of bets that go into the pot throughout the hand. Make sure to keep your tally running through each betting round. Don't get sidetracked, as so many players do, with the actual amount of money in the pot.

For example, assume you're on the button with K♥ 10♥. The big blind is already in the hand, so you start counting, "1, 2, 3," and so on, for each bet that goes into the pot. If there are six callers by time the action gets to you, and you decide to call, then you're getting pot odds of 6:1 with the small blind left to act. If he calls, you're getting pot odds of 7:1.

What if someone then raises? If everyone calls, there will be fourteen bets in the pot, not counting your two bets. This is a ratio of 14:2, which is the same as

7:1. What if it's reraised? If everyone calls again, there will then be twenty-one bets in the pot, not counting your three bets. This is a ratio of 21:3, which is still a ratio of 7:1. Listen to the dealer when all the action is completed before the flop. He'll announce the number of players still in the hand, which will help you keep the count straight. Continue counting the number of bets that go into the pot on the flop.

After the action on the flop is completed, you should recall the total number of bets in the pot, subtract one, and divide the resulting number by two. Why? Well, let's look at what you have to calculate.

The rake, the jackpot drop and the dealer's tip all come out of the pot, if you win it, so you subtract at least one bet to account for this loss. If you're playing in a $2/$4 game and the maximum rake is 10% up to $4, you should subtract two or even three bets from the preflop count. A $4 rake, a $1 jackpot drop and a 50¢ to $1 dealer tip is a lot to take out of a pot. It pays for you to be the one player in the game who knows to take this into account ahead of time.

Why divide by two? What we've played with before and on the flop are small bets, if you're playing in a $3/$6 or other structured game. The reason you now divide that number by two is that since the bet doubles from this point on, you now need to convert the count to big bets.

As an example, let's say there are twenty-eight bets in the pot after the flop. Twenty-eight bets minus one equals twenty-seven. Divide twenty-seven by two and you get thirteen-and-a-half big bets. I recommend you drop any fractions to give you a very slight cushion in your favor.

Now you've calculated that there are thirteen big bets in the pot. All you have to do is add one for each additional bet that goes in on the next two rounds. Your ultimate goal is to know how many bets are already in when you have to act on the river.

After your decision on whether to call to see the flop, the next most important decision you will make during the play of the hand will be whether to bet or call a bet on the river. Making decisions regarding betting for value and bluffing requires you to know exactly how many bets are in the pot at that point.

When there are no more cards to come, when you know exactly what the nuts are, when you know how close your hand is to the nuts, and when you have an idea of what your opponents' hands might be, you also need to know how many bets there are in the pot. That's because all mistakes are not created equal. A mistake on the flop might cost you one bet but a mistake on the river will cost you the entire pot.

How do the pot odds affect your play of a hand? The answer lies in the fact that you somehow have to connect your pot odds to the value of your hand. Let me start with a few simple examples to work toward answering that question.

You and I are going to flip a coin and bet on the outcome. Every time it comes up heads, you win, and I will pay you $1. Every time it comes up tails, I win, and you will pay me $1. How much money do you think you would be up after 20, 100 or 500 trials? The fact is, we'd be about even, especially as the number of trials increased. That's because this is a situation where the pot odds exactly equals the odds of winning the bet. Both of those odds are 1:1.

There's nothing I can do to improve my chance of winning this bet. So, how can I make money from it? The answer is that I have to change the odds that I'm being paid when I win a bet. If you now paid me $2 every time I won the bet, and I still paid you $1, I'd be a winner in the long run.

After 500 trials, we would each have won 250 times. I would have paid you $250, but you would have paid me $500. I would be a net $250 ahead. That's because I was getting pot odds of 2:1, when my chances of winning the hand were 1:1. The only thing that changed were the pot odds.

Suppose I was betting on the role of a single die (where the outcome has to be a 1, 2, 3, 4, 5 or 6). I'm betting that the role will come up a 6. If I bet $1 on each roll of the die, with no odds, I will lose the bet five times for every one time I win. The odds against me are 5:1. If I could get you to pay me $6 every time I win, I would break even in the long run. Obviously, I need the odds to pay better than the actual odds of winning the bet in order to get ahead.

How does this relate to poker odds? Suppose you have two hearts, and you get two more on the flop. You know that the odds of making the flush are about one out of three, or 2:1. For your flush draw to be profitable, the pot must be paying you odds of better than 2:1.

Keep in mind, though, that this calculation assumes that making the flush is the only way you can win. In real life, you'll often win without making the flush. Either you'll pair one of your hole cards, or you'll make a backdoor straight, or by you'll just have the highest card at the end of the hand. Maybe you'll even just bet as a bluff and not get called.

If you flop a four-flush, you have nine outs. Your exact chances of making the hand are 35%, or slightly better than 2:1 against. If you flop an open-end straight draw, you have eight outs, and your chances of making the straight are 31.5%, slightly worse than 2:1 against. I tell you this because practically speaking, you can look at both of these draws as having the same odds: 2:1 against. You have to do some rounding off in the actual game.

POT ODDS

If your opponent bets $6 and you're going to call, you have to call $6, not the $5.82 or the $6.13 that your hand might theoretically be worth. In most instances, "close enough" is good enough if you know that's your situation.

Recall the chapter on dominated hands. Many of the dominated hands were 4:1 underdogs–their chances of winning against the other hand were only between 18% and 21%. I'll bet that chapter left you with the impression that you should never play one of these hands, right?

Notice, though, that I carefully and deliberately did not make any recommendations about playing or not playing the hands. I want you to know that most of those dominated hands are great hands to play–under the right conditions. What do you think I mean by "the right conditions?" I mean that you have to have the right pot odds to play the hand.

If you're playing a hand that's a 4:1 underdog, you need pot odds of at least 4:1 just to break even in the long run. You might call a bet and lose four times, but then you'll win those bets back on the fifth time, when you win the hand (on average, in the long run).

Playing to break even in the long run is, of course, not exactly the way to play winning poker. You always want more than the bare minimum number of necessary bets in the pot in order to play a hand. Extra bets mean better pot odds. Having better pot odds is called an overlay. As a poker player, you're always looking for a spot to put your money in play where you have an overlay. If you stick to playing good, high cards for your position, and you play in a game where you can consistently get five or more players to play most pots, you're practically guaranteed to have a positive hourly rate and be a winner in the long run.

It's okay to play hands that have big odds against them as long as the pot is offering even bigger odds. If you hold a small pocket pair, your odds of flopping another same card to make a set are about 1 in 8. That's 7:1 against. If you add in the fact that you can win the hand a few other ways without flopping the set, you'll win the hand about 1 out of 3 times. Those are odds of 2:1.

In this situation, you need two other players in the hand to get the right odds to play the hand and break even in the long run. If you have three other players in the hand, you have a slight overlay, but it may not be enough to overcome the effect of the rake, the jackpot drop and your relative inexperience at the game. In other words, if you play the hand, you risk being out-played and losing to a better player, when you might have won the hand against weaker players.

I strongly recommend that you don't play small pocket pairs unless you're getting pot odds of at least 5:1. This strategy will save you a lot of losing hands and a lot of fluctuation in your bankroll. When you do win a hand, it'll be a good-sized pot, because you made sure of that before you called the first bet.

Don't forget that flopping a good hand doesn't necessarily mean that you'll win. Not only do you need the right odds to play a hand, you need to cushion those odds to allow for the fact that you'll sometimes make the hand and then lose with it. It's very expensive to be holding A♦ K♦, get two more diamonds on the flop, get the fifth diamond on the turn, make the nuts, and then lose the hand when the board pairs on the river.

I don't give too much thought to padding the odds (requiring grossly excess odds) when I hold two big cards, but I'm a stickler about it when I play smaller cards. I like to play hands like 8♥ 7♥, or especially 6♠ 5♠ (now named for me because I won two tournaments with that hand), but I play them only in late position with a lot of players in the hand. If there are seven or more players in the hand, I'll usually raise before the flop to build a big pot in case I hit my hand.

This is a profitable move for me, because I'm getting great pot odds and I, unlike a lot of other players, can throw the hand away on the flop if I miss. Since I was going to play the hand for one bet anyway, the move actually cost me only one bet, and I know I'll get that bet back in the same situation in the long run.

Some of my opponents complain openly and bitterly that I "play garbage hands" and I "don't play anything like [I] recommend in my first book" when I beat them with small cards. What they fail to notice is that I only play those hands when I'm in late position and getting great pot odds. I usually just drag the pot without saying anything, and I have never, ever pointed this out to them. Until now.

Test Your Knowledge #6
If you somehow knew for certain that your
sole opponent held A♥ A♦,
which two cards would you pick to give you
the best statistical chance to beat him,
if you played to the end of the hand?
Answer at the end of the chapter.

If you've played in a few hold'em games, you've undoubtedly noticed that it's not pocket aces or kings that win every hand. Usually, it's a hand that you wouldn't bet on every time, like K♥ 9♣, Q♣ 3♣, or 5♠ 5♦. No hand is totally worthless, it's just that some are obviously worth more than others.

Given the right circumstances, almost any hand can be an underdog. Even pocket aces are not a favorite if there are more than six players in the hand. The secret, the one thing that makes it alright to play an apparently bad hand, the great equalizer, is pot odds.

Test Your Knowledge #7
The reigning Super Bowl champions right now are the New England Patriots (Fall, 2002). The UCLA Bruins are a good college football team, but, if these two teams were to play each other, and each team played their best game, the college team would almost never win a game. Can you think of any reason in the world why anyone would ever bet on the Bruins in an honest game? I know this is not a poker question. I'm testing your ability to see the big picture.

Answers to Test Your Knowledge Questions #5-7

5. Your odds are 1.33:1, or 4:3.

6. The cards you should choose are the 6♣ 5♣ or the 6♠ 5♠. You will win 22.89% of the time. There are no two other cards that will win that often against pocket aces. You will win all club and spade flushes, you will win when there are four clubs or four spades on the board, and your 6 will steal a win when the board has a wheel.

7. The answer has to be pot odds. If the Bruins are expected to win (for example) only one time in fifty, then the odds on your bet have to be greater than 50:1. For every $1 you bet on the underdog, you'd have to be paid more than $50 for this bet to be profitable for

you in the long run. (50:1 and $50 are just an example, not any actual odds).

Structure Your Learning

Assignment #21

This book is intended for beginners, so I didn't develop graduate course level material on odds for you to memorize. Mainly, I just want you to see that you can profitably play hands that are obvious underdogs if you know in advance that you'll be adequately compensated for them. Many other poker books can provide you with more detailed explanations of pot odds and lots of examples. This chapter is just intended to begin your education on pot odds.

Next time you play in your usual game, think about the times that you would usually have played a hand but are now folding before the flop, because you read this chapter. Pay attention to those hands, and estimate how much money you saved when you folded. After the game, convert that number to big bets per hour. Compare the result to the one or two big bets per hour that a winning player hopes to win in the long run. I think you will be pleasantly surprised.

PLAYING ON THE TURN

Decisions made when you see the turn card are often routine and automatic. By this point, you'll have one of three types of hands:

1. Weak pairs, busted draws, and any hand that's obviously beat and doesn't have the right odds to play.

2. The probable best hand (could be an overpair, top pair with top kicker, a set or a completed hand).

3. A draw to the probable best hand with the right odds to continue (could be an open-end straight draw or a nut flush draw).

The way to play any of these hands is fairly straightforward. If you have a lousy hand, fold if there's a bet and wait for the next hand. If you have the probable best hand, then you should bet to get value from your hand and eliminate players. If you have a draw to the probable best hand, you'll usually check and call.

Because the bets double on the turn, a bet or a raise will force out the weaker hands, especially if the pot is small and they're not getting the right odds to call. The turn is when the undecided hands will fold rather than call a big bet. If you're equally undecided between betting or checking, you should usually opt for the bet. Betting greatly increases the chance you'll win the hand; often you'll do so right there on the turn.

If you already have a good hand on the turn, one with which you'd definitely call a bet, you should occasionally consider raising, even though it's not a bona fide raising hand. Since you'll probably have to put one big bet in on the turn and another one in on the river, sometime you can manage to put them both in at once on the turn. This play turns out to be especially profitable if your hand improves on the river. You've gotten in an extra bet with a winning hand and made the second-best hands pay more to try to beat you.

If you're drawing to a straight or a flush, and you make the hand on the turn, you should usually bet it right out into the players you were formerly checking to. Worried that you'll be giving away your hand? You are. That's not a problem, though.

The later it is in the hand, the more important it is that you win the pot right there. You don't need to disguise your hand anymore. The other players will either have the right odds to chase you down, or they won't. Make them pay no matter what they have.

PLAYING ON THE TURN

Realize that if you check on the turn, especially if everyone else has already checked to you, you're giving your opponents not one, but two free cards. They get to check with you on the turn, *and* they get to see the river card without putting any more money in the pot. Again, if you can think of any good reason at all to bet on the turn, you should do so. Free cards are something that your opponents are supposed to give you, not something you give them.

An easy way to understand the above advice is to realize that you're going to check and call when you have outs and bet when you don't. A flush draw is a hand that has outs, so you should usually check and call. When you make the flush, you no longer have any more outs, and now you should be betting. Same way with a straight draw.

The above advice notwithstanding, the turn represents an excellent opportunity for you to vary your play. A great deal of the time, you'll be folding on the turn. It's a common play, and there's certainly no disgrace in folding. Even better is to check, act like you're going to fold, and then instead raise when the action gets back around to you.

If you can make that check-raise play as often as one-third of the time you have a playable hand, you'll be training your opponents to check behind you when you check, because they fear a check-raise. Then, those times when you check with a bad hand, you'll often get a free card, because everyone will also check, thinking they're depriving you of a chance to check-raise.

Structure Your Learning

Assignment #22

The next time you play in your usual game, keep track of your play on the turn. Note whether you call or fold and whether your play turns out to be the right move. Count only those times when there's a bet on the turn and the winner (even if it's you) shows his hand on the river. Hands which don't go to the river, hands in which the winner is not called on the river, and hands in which everyone checks on the turn should not be part of this survey.

You should have four categories of entries in your notes:

1. You folded and it was the right decision (FY).
2. You folded and it was the wrong decision (FN).
3. You called and it was the right decision (CY).
4. You called and it was the wrong decision (CN).

You can prepare ahead of time by making the FY, FN, CY, and CN entries in your notebook, so you'll only have to make a mark under the right entry after each hand is over. If you have space and time, and can do it without drawing undue attention to yourself at the table, record why you made the wrong decision when you do. Analyze your mistakes–do you call or fold too often?–and if you can, correct them. Good luck.

CHECK-RAISING

Check-raising is not a big part of the game. When you're in first position with a good hand, and you're genuinely undecided between betting for value and trying for a check-raise, you should usually go ahead and bet. Don't try to get fancy. You'll make the most money just by playing your hand in a straightforward manner. Bet when strong, check when weak.

That said, check-raising can be useful in certain situations, so it's important to know how this tactic works. Check-raising is designed to do one of two things:

1. Force players to fold if they don't want to call two or more bets cold.

2. Trap players for an extra bet after they have already called a bet.

To visualize how check-raising works, try a simple exercise. Imagine that there are four players in a game and you're in the big blind. The small blind folded, so you're Player #1, the player on your left is Player #2, the player across from you is Player #3, and the player on your right, and on the button, is Player #4. Because of the preflop action, you happen to know that Player #3 has a good hand and will bet or raise on the flop. The focus of this exercise, though, is Player #2.

When the flop comes, you can act in one of two ways:

1. You bet, and Player #2 calls. When Player #3 raises, everyone calls, including Player #2. Player #2 has now called two bets.

2. You check. Player #2 also checks and Player #3 bets. When the action gets back to you, you raise (you just check-raised) and Player #2, faced with the prospect of calling two bets cold, probably folds.

With your check-raise, you've just knocked out an opponent who probably had a mediocre hand and didn't want to call two bets at once.

Here's a list of points to keep in mind when you're thinking about check-raising:

1. Let your big, overall objective in the hand be your guide. Do you want players to fold, or do you want them in the hand so you can trap them for extra bets?

2. If someone check-raises you, and it's unexpected, pause and take a moment to think about what it might mean. Does the other player *want* you to call two bets cold, or is he worried that you'll call one bet and then another if he just bets?

> *Test Your Knowledge #8*
> If the flop is Q♠ 7♣ 2♥, and someone check-raises to make you fold, what do you think he probably has? If he wants you to call the two bets, what do you think he has? Answer at the end of the chapter.

3. If you are check-raised on the flop, let the hand go if you've already got one bet in and you think you're beat. Too many players will automatically go ahead and call that extra bet without thinking about it. Resist the temptation to go on automatic pilot just because you want to see one more card. Players who can fold in this situation will plug a major leak in their game and add substantially to their hourly rate.

4. Pay attention when there's a raise before the flop. After the flop, you may want to remember exactly where that player is sitting in relation to you. You may need him to help you with a check-raise. After the flop, no one at the table, including the dealer, is allowed to say who raised earlier.

5. If you're going to check-raise, you might think that you need a 50-50 chance that someone else will bet when you check. You actually need a much better chance than that. You need to factor in the possibility that you will be reraised, and you also need to allow for those times that you check-raise and lose the hand. If you're a beginning player, I recommend that you hold yourself to a standard of "virtually certain" that there'll be a bet if you check.

6. When you're in late position or on the button against a lot of players, and everyone has checked to you, be aware that someone out there is probably waiting to check-raise you. The more players there are in the hand, the less likely it is that they all have checking hands.

7. A check-raise on the turn means something different than a check-raise before the flop or on the flop. A player who allows you to call one bet and then check-raises you on the turn knows that you need to see only one more card to make your hand and that, in all probability, you'll call. That player, therefore, always has a great hand. Learn to fold more often in this spot.

8. If you're check-raised and you don't know what to do, remember that you do know two things: you know what your hand is, and you know that the other player's hand is either better or worse than yours. All you have to do is decide whether he could be playing this way with a hand worse than yours.

9. Don't forget that you can check-raise when you're on a draw. If you have the nut four-flush draw or an open-end straight draw, you can check-raise if you're getting the right odds. Trapping five or more players for an extra bet when you have one of these hands is a great move. It will show a big profit in the long run and have a hugely positive impact on your hourly rate.

10. If you have a set or a completed hand, you can obviously beat one big pair or two pair. If a card comes on the end that could possibly make the other players two pair, especially if it's an ace, I'd definitely go for the check-raise.

For example, if you hold 10♠ 9♣, the board is J♥ 8♠ 3♠ 7♦, and you get the A♥ on the river, another player could very possibly have made aces and jacks or aces and 8s. He could even be holding A♣ K♣ and have made top pair with top kicker. Why don't you occasionally give another player a chance to bet in this situation? Check, so he'll bet. When he does, raise him.

Be a little more careful if the river card is a king. If you play mostly high cards, as I recommend, you'll often be in a position where a king on the river could make someone else a straight. If you hold 10♠ 9♣, and the board is Q♥ J♦ 3♠ 7♣, a king on the river will make you a straight, but anyone holding A10 will beat you.

Answer to Test Your Knowledge Question #8

With a flop of Q♠ 7♣ 2♥, there's no straight or flush draw out there. So the player check-raising you must have a hand worth betting and protecting. The question is, does he have a good hand and is therefore check-raising to get extra value from it, or does he have a hand that's good on the flop, but vulnerable?

If he's in early position, he's probably holding good cards, like A♥ Q♥, and betting for value. If he's in late position, he might have something like Q♦ 10♣, and be hoping to win the hand right there. He might also be holding 7♥ 7♦ or 2♠ 2♣ in late position and be betting for value. It helps to know your players. In any event, he's not bluffing and he's not on a draw.

Structure Your Learning

Assignment #23

Check-raising is a tactic that you won't use much in an average, low limit game. It's usually more profitable for you to stick to a solid, straightforward way of playing, especially when you're a beginner. When the other players at the table are, on average, better than you, any attempt to get fancy will often backfire. Plus, you won't always be able to count on someone else's betting if you check with the intention of raising.

You can, however, put yourself in a position where you'll have the best chance of pulling off a successful check-raise. I'm going to give you four similar, but separate, exercises to perform to teach you how to check-raise successfully.

CHECK-RAISING

You are to perform each of these exercises only when you are in early position and there are four or more players left to act behind you. You may decide for yourself what constitutes early position. You are to perform only one of the exercises for each time you play a regular-length session in your usual game. Your results will be easier to interpret if you do not mix these exercises together during the same playing session.

Again, only when you are in early position and there are four or more players to act behind you, you can try one of the following:

1. Try for a check-raise on the flop when you believe you've flopped the best hand. I would say that for a hand to qualify as the best hand, it should be no worse than top pair with top kicker or a pocket overpair to the flop. Top two pair, a set, and any completed hand obviously all qualify as the best hand.

Do this for an entire playing session, and try to estimate how much more money you won by check-raising. When you get home and you're completing your notes for the game, convert that amount into big bets per hour and mention it in your notes.

2. Try for a check-raise on the turn, observing the same criteria as you used on the flop, in Exercise 1. Again, estimate your extra win, convert it into big bets per hour, and add it to your notes.

3. Try for a check-raise on the flop, but only when you flop the nut four-flush draw, an open-end straight or what you believe is the probable best hand. When you're in one of the blinds, you'll often have nonstandard cards and be lucky enough to flop an unusual two pair or better. These hands count as probable best hands. Estimate your extra win, convert it to big bets per hour, and write it in your notes.

4. Follow the same guidelines as those in Exercise 3, but this time practice them on the turn instead of on the flop. Estimate your extra win, convert it to big bets per hour, and make it part of your notes.

If the only time you ever attempted to check-raise in the future was when you were in one of the four situations described above, you'd have very good results and your hourly rate would probably increase substantially. As you gain experience and become a more accomplished hold'em player, you can loosen up your check-raising requirements a little. Don't be too loose, though; it doesn't pay to play fancy. Stick with what you know best. Good luck.

BLUFFING

One pleasant Saturday morning this past spring, I was cleaning out my garage, when my son Neil came in and said, "Dad, I need to borrow the car. I have to go to the library to do some research for a term paper due at school." I gave him the keys to the car and off he went.

A few hours later, I was through cleaning up, and I went down to the mall to do some shopping. Well, guess who I ran into down at the mall?

"Neil," I said, "I thought you were going to the library."

"Dad, I was bluffing!" he replied. It didn't work for me when I was his age, but it did work for him. They say timing is everything.

In poker, **bluffing** means betting with a hand that you know cannot win if your bet is called. Players will often attempt to bluff when they're in the position of having a good flush or straight draw that didn't get there. They're trying to win the pot by making another player fold what they believe is a better hand.

Knowing when you should attempt a bluff is often just a simple matter of knowing the pot odds on the river and having an idea of what's in your opponent's hand. The mathematical rule of thumb for attempting a bluff is: *the pot odds must be greater than the odds of successfully pulling off the bluff.* For example, if you estimate that you have a 1 in 5 chance of bluffing and winning, there must be more than five bets in the pot when you attempt the bluff.

To start with, let's look at an example of how you would break even in the long run when bluffing:

Assume there are five bets in the pot, and you bet on the river as a bluff because you know you can't win any other way. If your opponent calls and beats you, you're losing one bet in attempted bluff situations. If you do this four more times, and lose all four of those times, you'll have lost five bets in attempted bluff situations. If you try it a sixth time, and this time you win the pot, you get back those five bets, along with your bet from the sixth bluff.

If there are ten bets in the pot, you can attempt to bluff ten times and lose all ten, as long as you win the pot on the eleventh try, on average. The end result is the same as unsuccessfully bluffing twenty times and then winning the next two times you bluff. You'll break even in the long run, as long as the pot odds are the same as your chances of successfully bluffing.

The way to make a profit from bluffing is to have pot odds that are greater than your chances of winning the hand. What if I slightly modified the first example, where you had a 1 in 5 chance of bluffing successfully? What if there were ten bets in the pot, instead of five? Well, you'd now have to invest (lose) five bets, and then you'd win ten bets when you won the hand. You'd lose four out of five times, but you'd be ahead five bets in bluffing situations overall. That's what pot odds will do for you.

On the other hand, what if there were only two bets in the pot when you attempted a bluff? You'd invest five bets on losing bluffing attempts and, and you'd win only two of those bets back when your bluff succeeded. Clearly, you should not attempt a bluff when the pot is not offering you the right odds. You'll really still be losing even though you might win one particular hand.

Now that you know that the pot has to be offering you the right odds to make bluffing worthwhile, there's another important question we have to address: How do you know what your odds of successfully bluffing are? How do you know if you have only a 5% chance of bluffing successfully, and you therefore need twenty or more bets in the pot? Or how do you know that you have a 33% chance of bluffing and therefore you need only two or more bets in the pot? This question is difficult to answer, precisely because it depends on your experience, your skill at reading your opponents' hands, and your estimation of what all the earlier action means and even of who the other players are.

You cannot bluff bad players, because they are not astute enough to recognize that you could be betting a good hand for value. They'll often call, expecting to lose the hand anyway, just because they play too loose and it's worth it to them to spend the extra bet on the end just to see your hand. This carelessness is what makes them bad players.

It's also hard to bluff good players, because they recognize bluffing opportunities, and they consider the fact that you could be bluffing when deciding to call. You also cannot bluff a player who has a good hand, but who you've misread for a busted straight or flush draw. All of the conditions have to be right to pull off a bluff, especially when you're trying to run it through more than one opponent.

There's a little bit more math to bluffing that you need to understand. It has to do with how many potential callers you have when you attempt to bluff. To see this point, assume that it's equally likely (50-50) that each player will call when you attempt to bluff on the end. If you're first and there's just one other player, the odds that you'll be successful are 50-50 (1/2), or 1:1. If there are two other players, you have odds of 1 out of 4 (1/2 x 1/2), or 3:1. Three players (1/2 x 1/2 x 1/2) makes odds of one out of eight, or 7:1. Four players is 15:1

against. Five players is 31:1 against. You can see how these odds against you increase exponentially. They get out of hand pretty quickly, which is exactly why bluffing works best against only a few players.

There's another factor that works against you when you're trying to bluff, especially when you're bluffing into more than two players. Beginning and low limit players sometimes feel that they're honor bound to call you with anything, especially as the last player in the hand who could keep you from winning the pot. The last player will often call your attempted bluff just because he's the last player, and not because he's considering pot odds or his poker hand.

Besides your opponents profiles, what else should you consider when deciding whether to bluff? Pot-size is an important factor in your analysis. Medium-sized pots are the most difficult to steal. Why? Well, there's a reason they got to be medium-sized. It's usually because an average number of players got average cards, made average-strength poker hands, and created an average-sized pot. If you try to bluff into one of these pots, you'll get called by an average hand.

Very small pots are the easiest to steal, because there's usually a very small number of players in those hands, most of whom will fold slightly better than average hands when you bluff, because they often correctly realize that they're not getting the right pot odds to call you.

Often, these players will have only one small bet invested in the pot. They don't want to call a big bet on the river, because there's little to win by risking so much. If you're interested in bluffing for a small pot, it helps if you keep the pot small by not betting on the flop, as long as you think it's safe to do so. You generally don't want to give free cards but, in those instances when it's correct to do so, one of the benefits is that it may help you successfully bluff on the river.

Very large pots can be very profitable to bluff for. The difference is that you may go a long time between winning these bluffs. When you do win one, though, the pot odds will more than compensate you for the times you lost. In summary, unless you have very good, specific reasons for bluffing at medium-sized pots, you should try to make most of your bluffing attempts at very small or very large pots.

Favorable Times To Bluff

I've identified ten instances in the game when you might (or should) be thinking about bluffing. Review this list occasionally to keep these points in your mind.

1. When you have AKs. If you raised before the flop and played the hand strongly from the beginning, your opponents will give you credit for a good hand. They may think you have AKs, AA or AK, or whatever two cards it takes to make a completed hand. If you don't make a great hand, a bluff attempt on the river may still work, because they don't realize you're bluffing.

2. When you have excellent pot odds. If you missed your draw on the river, and the pot is huge, you should at least give a thought to bluffing before checking and folding. Sometimes the pot is so big it's worth a try.

3. When you're playing against good players. An experienced player is capable of figuring out what you might be holding and give you credit for it. He will then make a mathematical calculation, and, if he doesn't have the right pot odds to call, he will fold. Bad players don't do this; they just call anyway.

4. When you have hidden strength. If you're in the blind with unusual cards, and you get a flop to match them, or if you've varied your play and hit a good flop, you have hidden strength. Your opponents often won't realize that a check from you means you have a strong hand (in this instance you're bluffing to pretend your hand is worse than it actually is, not better).

5. When you're in higher stakes games. These games have better players, who are capable of folding one pair or two pair when they think they're beat.

6. When the flop didn't hit anyone. If you read everyone in the hand as holding high cards and the flop is all low cards, you might be able to bluff for the pot.

7. When the board pairs on the turn. If the flop is K♦ 8♥ 3♣, and there is no bet, you can often steal the pot when another king comes on the turn. Someone with top pair would almost always have bet it on the

flop. In this case, you can be sure that no one has three kings, and your opponents will probably give you credit for them. Even if they think you might not have the kings, you've got them playing a guessing game, so they will often fold.

8. When you're playing against just one opponent. If I have to bluff for a pot, I always prefer to be facing only one opponent. It doesn't get any better than that. Well, actually, it does. Sometimes, when the river card comes and it's just you and one opponent, he'll fold and concede the pot out of turn if he totally missed his draw. But it doesn't get any better than that!

9. When you want to fake a rush. If your seat is hot and you've just won five of the last seven hands, you can sometimes bet with obvious (fake) confidence and hope your opponents will think you're still on the rush.

10. When you're in the blind. From the blind, you could have anything, and most players recognize that. Rather than play a guessing game, especially with a small pot, they will fold unless they have a better than average hand.

Unfavorable Times To Bluff

Take another look at the above list of favorable times to bluff. Now look at it from the other player's point of view. Everything you can figure out about the other players, they can also figure out about you. And there's only one of you to keep an eye on them, but there are nine of them to watch you. That's why it's so hard to get away with anything.

Here are some situations to beware of when thinking about a possible bluff:

1. Any flop with an ace. These flops are hard to bluff at because players just seem to play every time they get an ace. If one comes on the flop, it's very likely to have made someone a pair, so you'll certainly get called.

2. Any flop with a jack or a 10. These two cards are what all good straight draws are made of. Good players will usually have cards that would go well with jacks and 10s. You can practically forget about bluffing when there's both a jack and a 10 on the board.

3. If there was a preflop raise. This indicates that there are some premium hands out there, and you can't be sure that one of them isn't AA or KK (in which case you'll get called when you bluff on the river). Sometimes, a player will raise before the flop with 44 just for fun, and then call with it on the river—just for fun.

4. Many players in the hand. Yes, I've already mentioned this as a problem, but it's well worth keeping in mind all the time.

Your Opponent Might Be Bluffing If...

1. It seems like he missed a flush or straight draw. Maybe the flop had two cards of the same suit and another one did not come on the turn or the river. Or maybe there was an obvious straight draw that did not get there. In a case like that, his only option might be to try a bluff.

2. It's just the two of you. If he's first to bet, or if you're first and you check to him, he could be bluffing. He won't always be bluffing just because there are only the two of you, but it's something you should keep in mind.

3. It cost him only one bet to steal the pot. If your opponent can induce you to make a mistake that will cost you the pot, and he can do so for only one bet, clearly he'll want to try that.

4. The pot is huge. I'd say that any pot with more than fifteen big bets qualifies in most players' minds as a huge pot, and is worthy of a steal attempt.

5. The player betting on the river, who's therefore possibly bluffing, raised preflop and no aces, kings, or queens are on the board.

6. Everyone checked on any round of the hand. This usually means that no one flopped anything worth protecting.

8. When two or more of the above reasons to believe your opponent might be bluffing are both true, the more likely it is that he's bluffing.

Structure Your Learning

Assignment #24

The next time you play in your usual game, pay attention to the betting that takes place on the river. As you undoubtedly know by now, not every bet that is made on the river is made because the bettor has the nuts and is betting for value. A lot of those bets are going to be pure bluff attempts. But which ones? I will leave that for you to decide for yourself.

If you're in the hand on the river, and you find yourself saying, "I think that guy's bet is a bluff," under your breath, then here's what I want you to do:

1. Determine the pot odds. If you have to call $6 with a $55 pot, then you're getting pot odds of about 9:1. If you have to call $8 with a $45 pot, then you're getting pot odds of about 5.5:1, or 11:2.

2. Try to determine what your chances of winning the hand are in a showdown with the bettor. Say to yourself, "I have a 1 out of X chance of winning this hand." You decide what the X is.

3. Now compare the two numbers from steps 1 and 2. Remember, you want the number from step 1 to be bigger than the number from step 2. For example, you might say to yourself, "I think my chances of winning the hand are 1 out of 6, and the pot odds are 9:1." Or, "I think my chances of winning the hand are 1 out of 3, and the pot odds are 5:1."

4. If the number from the pot odds is bigger than the number you came up with from your hand, you should call. The pot is offering you better odds than you need, so you have an overlay. That's a great situation to be in, and you will show a profit in the long run, which will add to your hourly rate.

5. If you call this possible bluff because you have the right pot odds, keep track of how you make out. Every time you call to catch a possible bluff, count how many bets it costs you to call, and count how many bets are in the pots you win. If you call one bet and win a pot with eight bets in it, your count would be +8. Don't count the bet you called with.

If you call a possible bluff and lose the hand, however, then subtract one bet from your running count. Now you're at +7. If you try to catch three more bluffs and lose them all, your running count would be at +4. If you then catch a bluff with 15 bets in the pot, your running count would now be +19. Start this running count at the beginning of the game, and keep it going until your playing session is over. When you're completing your notes, make sure this count is in big bets (it should already be big bets, since you're counting only bets that take place on the river) per hour, and compare that number to the one or two big bets per hour that you hope to win in the long run.

BLUFFING

Remember that your running count is meant be a count of only the number of bets you win and lose, and not the number of times you make the bet or the number pots you win or lose. Count only the number of bets that go in and out of your stack of chips.

I recommend that you do not perform this exercise during the same playing session as the next exercise. Keep them separate. Even though they are both about bluffing, I think it will help keep you focused if you perform them on separate days.

Assignment #25

Now put the shoe on the other foot. Let's look at only those times you're in the pot on the river, you're first to bet, and you know that the only way you can win the hand is to bet as a pure bluff. These are the only hands we want to count for this exercise.

Again, you're going to keep a running count of the number of bets you win and lose when attempting to bluff. If you attempt to bluff and get caught, your running count is -1. If you try it six more times and lose all six of those times, your running count is down to -7. If you then bluff and win a pot with 25 bets in it, your running count is now up to +18. In this example, you can see that you attempted to bluff eight times, lost seven of those times and yet, you're a whopping 18 big bets ahead when it comes to bluffing! See what the power of pot odds can do for you? You always have to count the pot when you have an important decision to make. Whenever you see a player fold his hand while saying, "The pot's not big enough," you know that he's a player who understands pot odds.

The object of the above exercises is for you to have a positive running count in bluffing and catching bluffs. If you find that you're right virtually every time that you decide to snap off a suspected bluff, you're not calling enough in those situations. Loosen up and call a little more often in those spots. Conversely, if you succeed almost every time you try to bluff, you're definitely not bluffing enough. If it works almost every time, why don't you try bluffing a little more often?

Don't go overboard, though. When I'm in a spot where the pot odds are only slightly favorable, I usually pass! If I need odds of 8:1 and I'm getting 9:1, for example, I'll usually fold as if the odds were slightly worse than what I need rather than slightly better (as they are).

Why? Well, close calls cause you to have big fluctuations in your bankroll without adding substantially to your overall winnings or hourly rate. I realize that I might be giving up a very slight mathematical edge but I simply don't like fluctuations in my bankroll. I just like to see it steadily grow with each passing hour in the game.

READING HANDS

Maybe you've noticed that most of my advice on how to play relies on your having an idea of what your opponents are holding. By now you're probably asking, "How can I know what they have with any certainty?" Don't worry. It's possible to figure out what they have, and sometimes their hands will even be quite obvious, but knowing your opponents' hands usually requires you to take in a lot of different information correctly and quickly and arrive at a conclusion in time to play your hand without holding up the game.

If you're trying to read another player's hand, some of the questions you might ask yourself are:

1. What do I already know about this player?
2. Has he played a hand like this before?
3. What position is he in?
4. Is he in the blind?
5. Did he raise before the flop?
6. Did he call a raise before the flop?
7. Did he check-raise on any round of the hand?

8. Did he call a check-raise?

9. How does he react to other players' bets and raises?

10. Have I picked up any tells from this player?

11. Statistically speaking, what are the odds that he holds the hands that I think he might hold?

12. Why did he raise before the flop, on the flop, or on the turn or river?

13. Why *didn't* he raise before the flop, on the flop, or on the turn or river?

14. If I put myself in his place, and I played the hand the way he has from the beginning, what would I have?

15. What are his pot odds?

16. What does my common sense, experience and logic tell me he might have?

These are a lot of questions to ask and answer in a short amount of time (in the heat of the battle, no less!), and they're only a sample of the many questions that could be asked. Fortunately, many hands are similar in the way that they're played, and the fact that you might play hundreds of hands per playing session will give you plenty of practice reading similar hands.

Of all the skills required to be a good hold'em player, the ability to read hands is one of the most time-consuming and difficult to master. It requires that you play or watch many, many hands, and that you expend the mental energy necessary to work through each hand, so you arrive at correct conclusions. It also requires that you pay attention to the game and the players in progress even when you're not in the hand, which is something that the average low limit player doesn't usually do. And all of this assumes that you started with a good, solid, practical and theoretical understanding of all of the other aspects of the game.

If you already play in a regular game, the good news is that you already have some practice reading hands, even if you're not yet an expert at it. You already know about all of the possible combinations of questions you can ask about the play of a hand, and about the many different situations that can arise. Fortunately, many of these situations and questions are so similar that they can be reduced to a manageable number that will give you a satisfactory conclusion most of the time.

Because of the huge number of variables involved in reading hands, the impossibility of covering every feasible combination of events in the play of a hand, and the fact that this is intended to be a beginner's book, I'm going to help you learn how to read hands by asking you to accomplish the following assignment.

Structure Your Learning
Assignment #26
There's a principle in teaching that says that if you're going to teach someone something, one of the very first things you have to do is determine what the student already knows about the subject. This ensures that the student and the teacher are "on the same page," and that they begin the lesson in the appropriate place. In this lesson, you get to decide exactly what your level of competence is, and we will start at that point.

The next time you play in your usual game, pay attention to those times that a player bets and is called on the river. It doesn't matter if you're in the hand or not. If you've been following the action from the beginning, and you've been trying to read that player's hand, I want you to come up with an educated guess of what his hand might be.

It will help you if you decide at the beginning of the hand to use that hand as part of this assignment. I want you to tell yourself exactly which two cards the player might be holding. For example, if the board is Q♣ J♠ J♥ 6♦ 2♠, and you think he has a full house, don't just say, "I think he has a full house." Instead, say, "I think he has pocket 6s," or, "I think he has Q♦ J♦."

When the player in question is called on the river and he reveals his hand, you'll see that your guess will, of course, fall into one of three categories:

1. You'll have guessed that his hand is worse than it is. 2. You'll have guessed that his hand is better than it is. 3. You'll have been right on the mark.

Be prepared by having these three categories already written in your notes, and make a mark in the appropriate category. If you have time and space, also try to jot down why you think your guess was too high or too low. Review your notes later, when you have time to reflect on what you wrote. Hopefully, you can learn a bit more about reading hands from these notes. Your goal, of course, is to have more and more of your guesses be right with each passing playing session.

Don't be too hard on yourself. If the board is 9♦ 8♥ 7♣ 2♠ 2♥, and you think the player has 8s full of 2s, I would count it as a correct guess if he in fact held pocket 9s or 7s instead of the 8s. However, if you think he holds 9♥ 2♣ to make the full house, and he actually has pocket 8s, I'd count that as guessing too low. Remember, it's his pocket cards you're trying to guess, not just his final poker hand.

SHORT-HANDED GAMES

A short-handed game is one that has either three, four, or five players. If you're watching a short-handed game in progress for the first time, it will look like a wild and crazy mess, with the calling, betting and raising not making any apparent sense at all.

If you see the players in a short-handed game raising all the time with questionable cards, calling with even worse cards, betting with nothing, giving their opponents no respect, and being extremely proud of their ace-high or pair of 4s at the end of the hand, you know you're watching a game that is full of players who are experts at short-handed play.

The ability to play in a short-handed game and maintain a positive hourly rate, especially over a long period of time, is one of the most difficult achievements in hold'em. Short-handed play is a very advanced skill that requires an extensive knowledge of game theory, backed up with countless hours of real-life playing experience. Short-handed games are not made for beginners. If you're contemplating taking a seat in a short-handed game, the very most important thing you need to know is exactly what the skill levels are of the players already in the game.

I've already mentioned the saying: "Poker is not a game of cards played with people; rather, it is a game of people played with cards." It's very true. You're not playing against cards, you're playing against people. So take a minute to look at the people that you're considering playing against.

When you play in a poker game, you're really pitting your decision-making abilities against those of all of your opponents combined. When you play in a short-handed game, you'll be playing a lot more hands than you would in a full game. You might even be playing almost every hand. With all those opportunities to make a decision (and therefore possibly a bad decision), you might lose your bankroll in short order.

There's one time when you might find yourself in a good short-handed situation: if you've been playing in your usual game and the other players start to drop out, one by one, without more players taking their seats. Perhaps it's getting later at night, and there are no names on the list.

Often what will happen is that the game will become seven- or eight-handed, one of the players will say, "I don't want to play if it's only seven-handed," and he'll leave. His departure will trigger the same reflex in another player and the game will suddenly be five-handed. After a few hands, the game will often break up, because three other players will each say, "I don't want to play five-handed."

If this happens in your usual game, and you're playing against your usual opponents, then those hands before the game breaks up provide an excellent opportunity for you to practice your short-handed skills, particularly if you feel that the other players' short-handed game is not much better than yours, and especially if you think that they don't even know of the differences between a full and a short-handed game. Do what you can to keep the game from breaking up so you can take advantage of this chance.

Here's a list of points to keep in mind if you find yourself in a short-handed game:

1. Players whose usual style of play is loose and aggressive will unknowingly be playing a good game when it's short-handed. Short-handed play is characterized by continuous, unrelenting betting and raising, so players who already play that way will have a leg up on the game.

2. You should change your playing style from tight-aggressive to mostly loose-aggressive. If you play your usual tight game, the blinds will eat you up, and you'll be folding before the flop too often.

3. Big cards are worth more. AK, KJ, and QJs will win without much improvement against three players more often than they will against nine players.

4. Because big hands win more easily, you can raise preflop with many more hands than you would in a full game. If you have a good handle on the other aspects of a short-handed game, you can usually raise preflop any time both of your cards are an 8 or above.

5. Because there's a lot of preflop raising when it's short-handed, you should always raise before the flop when you hold AA, KK, QQ, AKs, and other big cards. Since players expect that you'll raise anyway, the raise actually helps disguise your strength.

6. Forget that your cards are suited, if they are. It doesn't take a flush to win every time. In fact, you don't have to try to make flushes or straights, because two high cards will often be enough to win. Usually, you won't be getting the correct odds to draw to a flush or straight, but that's no problem, since you're really betting on just the high rank value of your cards.

7. Because most pots will be raised before the flop, small pairs and suited connectors go way down in value. It costs a lot of money to call a raise with 7♦ 6♦, flop a draw, and pay to draw, only to miss the draw or make a pair of 6s on the river. Think ahead.

8. Do not routinely play hands with a 2, 3, or 4 in them. That's like playing with only one card, because you'll always get overcards. Again, think ahead.

9. Don't forget to gear it up a notch. Call when you might normally fold with that marginal hand. Raise when you would ordinarily just call. Reraise a little more liberally. Check-raise more often. Call more often on the river with what would be a weak or second-best hand in a full game.

10. Ask for a rake break and a single blind. If they say you can't play for the jackpot when the rake is reduced, tell them, "Great!" As you may recall from the chapter on jackpots, the odds are really against hitting the jackpot in a short-handed game. Why give a dollar per hand to the players in the full game who will hit the jackpot? A single blind helps you because it keeps you from having to play garbage hands as often.

11. Being able to play well in a short-handed game is a must-have skill if you're going to be a tournament player. If you're going to place high in a tournament, you'll eventually have to learn how to play when the table is short-handed, so it's worth developing this skill when you have the chance.

12. Before you play in any short-handed game, truthfully and honestly evaluate your short-handed skills. Compare them to those of your potential opponents.

13. Gaining skill at short-handed play will definitely help you in your usual full game. Many times almost everyone will fold in a full game. At that point it's as if you're playing short-handed, especially if you're in late position. Consider what you know about playing in late position, stealing the blinds and reading players.

If you decide to play in a short-handed game, it should usually be for one of two reasons:

1. You know you'll be one of the best players in the game, so you think you'll have a positive hourly rate.

2. You know that you won't one of the best players in the game, but the other players aren't that much better than you are, and you see this as a good opportunity to gain some experience without risking too much.

If you can't meet one of those two criteria, wait for a better chance to put your money in action. In either case, don't play unless you know what you're doing.

Structure Your Learning

Assignment #27

Practice playing in short-handed games according to the guidelines I've mentioned in this chapter. Keep separate records of your results in these games, and if possible, name the other players in your notes. This will help you more accurately evaluate your prospects when faced with future short-handed playing opportunities. Good luck.

TOURNAMENTS

Other than jackpots, one way that the average low limit hold'em player can score a big win and really increase his hourly rate is by winning or placing high in a poker tournament. Sometimes, in a tournament, you can win more than $1,000 in just three hours of play. Studying tournament strategy is also very valuable to you because it speeds up your learning process and helps you play in your regular ring (full) game.

There's a big difference between tournament and ring game strategy. A player who is good in his regular ring game will almost never win a tournament if he uses his ring game strategy throughout the tournament. There are so many differences that tournament strategy has been discussed in numerous books devoted entirely to that subject.

For the sake of your basic hold'em education, I've outlined below what should be some of your important considerations if you're thinking about playing in a hold'em tournament:

1. Should you play in a particular hold'em tournament? I play tournaments, and I choose which ones I play in for two possible reasons. Either I believe that I have a reasonable chance to make the final table (get in the money), or I think that the practice and experience I will get by entering this tournament will be worth the entry fee. There are many good tournaments with $5/$20 entry fees that are worth the experience.

2. The number one difference between a ring game and a tournament is that in a tournament, survival is what it's all about. In a ring game, you can voluntarily play many dominated hands, because you can lose five hands in a row and make it all back on the sixth hand. If you run out of poker chips before you win that sixth hand, you can always buy more. You can't do that in a tournament, because one or two hands could take all of your chips and you cannot buy any more.

3. If you're playing in a tournament that allows rebuys and add-ons, be prepared to make the maximum number of rebuys and add-ons. Tournaments like this are as much a contest to see who can buy the most chips as they are a contest to win those chips. You need to be able to keep up with the competition just to have a chance to make the final table.

4. Each player's stack size is of paramount importance in a tournament. You should not ordinarily attack a bigger stack than yours because if you lose the hand, you could be eliminated from the tournament, while

your opponents will only lose some chips to you and will remain in the tournament.

5. If it is a rebuy event, you can and should play a little more liberally during the rebuy period. You can afford to take chances in an effort to get ahead, and losing won't bust you out of the tournament.

6. Decide ahead of time exactly which hands you will play and under what circumstances. Decide which hands you'll use to call preflop raises.

7. Always be aware of your position relative to the button. It'll help you decide if another player is making a move based on his position more than his cards.

8. Always be aware of the other players' stack sizes, especially before the play of the hand. Players with small stacks are usually more reluctant to call your bets and raises if you act before they do on the hand.

9. Always be aware of how much time is left in the current stage of the tournament. Certain strategies become more effective near the end of each stage.

10. Always have an idea of how much the blinds and the antes will cost you to play each round. Use this to determine how many hands you have before you will be blinded out if you don't win a hand or make a move.

11. Pay attention to the cost of calling the rest of the small blind. Most of the time it's correct to fold.

12. Tighten up considerably after the rebuy period. You're playing for keeps. You can't replace chips you lose except by winning them back from other players.

13. Never miss an opportunity to put a player all-in. If your opponent bets ten of his eleven chips, and you have forty-five chips, you should always raise one more to get him all-in. You've probably heard the saying that all a player needs to beat you is a chip and a chair. It's true. Try to deprive him of both.

14. Don't underestimate the value of a single chip. Do not play too loose, wild or reckless in the beginning of the tournament, just because you have a lot of chips and the limits are small. Beginning players too often make this mistake.

15. Be aware of how many total chips are in play in the tournament, and of how many players there are left. With this information, you'll be able to determine the average number of chips for each player.

16. If you have a small stack late in the tournament, you must realize that you probably won't win. Your goal, therefore, is to end up as high on the payout ladder as you can. If other players have short stacks, give them every chance to bust each other out before you get blinded out.

17. The IRS requires casinos to issue a Form WG-2 to anyone in the tournament who receives $600 or more. If you're making a deal at the final table and you don't want a WG-2, you can ask for $599 or less and avoid the IRS paperwork.

18. Players who are eager to make a deal at the last table will probably play more conservatively than usual if their offer to make a deal is refused.

19. Traditionally, tournament players are not allowed to select their table or seat at that table. However, there are a few poker rooms that allow it, even though it may not be well known. Ask if you can choose your own seat and table. If you can, get a seat at what you know will be the final table. You'll be one of the few players in the tournament who won't be forcibly moved from table to table, so you may avoid paying double blinds and being in bad position.

20. Watch the best tournament player at your table, especially early in the tournament. Stay out of his way unless you have great cards.

Structure Your Learning
Assignment #28
Tournament experience can do a lot to help improve your regular ring game. You'll see that you really have to watch every hand carefully, and you'll learn a lot faster in a tournament that you would in a ring game.

Try to play in a few tournaments to gain experience, if for no other reason. I suggest you keep your tournament expenses and wins separate in your records. This chapter alone cannot turn you into a great tournament player—it's intended only to be an introduction to tournaments. If you're interested in learning more about tournament play, look for books devoted exclusively to tournaments.

LAST WORDS

Before I close this book and send you back to the hold'em table to practice, I'd like to point out a few features of hold'em which I don't particularly like. Perhaps you've found them similarly bothersome, and I may be able to help you find a way to deal with them.

Chopping

Imagine that you're in your usual good hold'em game and everything's going just great for you. Imagine that you're in the big blind. You look down at your hand and see that you have K♣ K♥. You look up to watch the action come around to you, and you see that everyone folds except the small blind.

Then the player in the small blind starts to cry. He looks at you, and with a trembling, whining, and piti-ful voice he says, "I don't have a good hand. I don't want to raise you to steal your blind because you might call. I don't want to call with this hand because it's a lousy hand. And I don't want to fold because I've got part of a blind bet out there and I don't want to lose that, either."

He pauses for a moment, and then he says, "I really don't know how to play in the small blind, so what I'd like you to do is just give me my money back, and let's go on to the next hand. However, if I did hold a good hand right now I'd be in there swinging, trying to win from you all the money I could with it."

Actually, the player in the small blind doesn't really say any of those things. All he does is smile at you and say, "Wanna chop?" To me, it's the same lousy thing.

I don't like **chopping** for a lot of good reasons:

1. It changes the rules in the middle of the game, at your opponent's discretion. It's as if you're playing with two sets of rules, and you don't know which set applies until after the small blind looks at his hand and decides which set is best for him. Players may ask if you want to chop when they have Q5 or 72; what do you think they do when they have AA or KQs?

2. It penalizes players who know how to play in the small blind. Poker is all about having skills that your opponents don't have. You've plugged that particular leak in your game. Why should you give money back to a player who's too lazy or too dumb to do the same?

3. You might have lost lots of money and taken years to learn how to play in the small blind. You paid your dues in that situation, and now it's your turn to recoup those losses from other players who don't know how to play in the small blind.

4. It rewards ignorance and laziness in a game where people literally bet that they know what they're doing. Players who can't or won't develop certain skills want their money back whenever they're confronted with situations they can't handle.

5. It deprives the big blind of the opportunity to play a good hand. If all of the other players have folded, it's more likely statistically that the remaining player–the big blind–has the cards necessary to make a good hand.

6. The player now in the big blind (that's you) was in the small blind last hand, and he played by the rules; why should this small blind ask for a break?

7. It deprives the big blind of his turn in the rotation to have position over at least one other player (the small blind) for an entire hand.

Chopping began as a favor the poker room did for the players to allow them to escape the rake when only two players were in the hand. Rather than having to rake a pot with just one small bet from both blinds (when both checked all the way to the river to avoid a higher rake), the poker room created chopping, which allows the two players to agree to take back their money and move on to the next hand. "No Flop; No Drop" is the underlying principle behind chopping.

Whenever the player on my right says, "Wanna chop?"

I'd like to turn to him and say, "I've taken the time and effort to improve my standards of poker playing. In particular, when it comes to playing in the small blind, I've really upped my abilities—up yours."

Having said all that, I do understand the arguments in favor of chopping. Chiefly, it avoids the rake and speeds up the game. I've given it some thought and analysis, and I've come up with what I think is the fairest possible answer to "Wanna chop?"

I think you should tell the questioner that you will agree to chop every time, or you will never chop at all. This keeps the other player from using chopping as an unfair advantage, and it helps keep you from being the one player in the game who refuses to chop.

I'd like to take this opportunity to appeal to poker room managers not to allow chopping in games where the pot is not raked when only both blinds are in the pot before the flop.

In other words, if you're in a $2/$4 game, only the blinds are in the hand (so there's only $4 in the pot), and the pot doesn't get raked until it reaches $5, chopping should not be allowed. On the other hand, if you're playing $15/$30, and a call from the small blind would obviously cause the pot to be raked, chopping should be allowed.

LAST WORDS

The Must-Move Rule

I currently live in the Kansas City area, where there's only one poker room in town. The have a must-move rule, which means that second and subsequent hold'em games are used as feeder games to ensure that the first game is always ten-handed and never runs out of players.

If you come in on Saturday, at first, you'll usually be seated in the fourth or fifth hold'em game (after a long wait). After playing in your game anywhere from thirty minutes to two hours, you'll be moved to the third game. Then you'll be moved to the second game. If enough players eventually leave the main game, you'll end up there.

Over the course of an evening, almost every player in a hold'em game gets forcibly moved from game to game, as the poker room attempts to ensure that every game except the last one is always full. This is a horrible way to treat customers. There's no good reason that a player should be forced to leave one game just to take a seat at another table, unless the game you're in actually breaks up due to lack of players.

The main problem I have with this rule is that it exists mainly for the convenience of the poker room, because it ensures that every pot is big enough to rake. It also forces every player who's playing Texas hold'em to play at a ten-handed table, and not every hold'em player likes that. I've been in the main game, which was full, and the poker room manager would not let me move over to the only other hold'em game in the room, which was seven-handed.

I've brought up this subject as a way to let you in on a little-known but powerful secret about Texas hold'em. If you're a good, solid player who might be a beginner but has a sound understanding of the game, full ten-handed games are bad for you! If you can stick to playing mostly high cards and playing only when you have the best of it, I believe that seven- and eight-handed games are the best for you.

Why? Well, most of the hands that you'll win pots with are going to be one pair (top pair with top kicker), two pair (often top two pair), and, occasionally, a set. The fewer players there are in the hand, the more likely it is that these lower ranking hands will hold up at the end. You can beat five or six other players consistently with these hands.

The problem is that these hands will survive six opponents, but they won't survive nine opponents. People say, "I want to play at a full, ten-handed table, because I want to be paid off very well when I make my winning hand." They don't realize that the extra bets put in the pots by the ninth and tenth players do not make up for the pots that the ninth and tenth players beat them out of. In other words, the added benefit of having their bets in a pot you win is not enough to make up for entire pots they cause you to lose.

LAST WORDS

You'll often be in a game where there are players in all ten seats, but some of the players are away from the table for one reason or another. They might be on dinner breaks, sidetracked by slot machines, at the bar, or who knows where. If there are only seven or eight players in your game, don't leave the game for any reason. This is a perfect situation for you. If you have to go anywhere, wait until your game becomes full again.

Most of the strategic moves that you've learned in this book, such as betting for value, raising, check-raising, and bluffing work best when there are a few players missing from the table. Of course, if the house rules allow you to move voluntarily from a full game to a six- or seven-handed game, I think you should do so.

Concluding Remarks

I didn't know it until several hundred other poker players graciously took the time to point it out to me over the past few years, but there's apparently an unwritten rule that if you're a poker writer, you can play only high limit poker. I'm often asked why I like to play in $3/$6, $4/$8, and $5/$10 hold'em games, and why I don't play in the highest limit games in the poker room.

There are a couple of reasons for my choices. The first one you already know—I don't like to see big fluctuations in my bankroll. Keeping in mind that my profit comes from the mistakes my opponents make, I like to play in games where they're making a lot of mistakes. The poker room I currently play in does not offer $10/$20 hold'em, which is what I'd really like to play most of the time if it were available. I also really enjoy playing the game, and I miss some of that enjoyment when playing at very high limits.

There's one reason, though, that's more important to me than any of the others. It has to do with the fact that I like to have a good chance of leaving a winner when I put in a playing session. Look at it this way—would you rather have a:

1. 100% chance of winning $100?
2. 50% chance of winning $200?
3. 33 1/3% chance of winning $300?
4. 10% chance of winning $1,000?

As you might quickly see, each of these equations represents a different level of risk and a different payoff, yet they all equal the same win: $100. Me, I'd rather have a 90% chance of winning $300 six times than a 75% chance of winning $2,300 one time.

By way of closing this book, I'd like to ask for your assistance. I have a few future book ideas in mind, but they're the type of books that I can't write without some help.

First, I'd like to hear what you think of this book, so I can possibly incorporate your ideas in my revisions in the future. I want this book to be as good as possible. If your ideas will help improve a hold'em student's hourly rate, I'd like to hear from you.

Everybody has a bad beat story. Some people have twenty of them. Nobody cares. Until now. I'd like to be the first person in the history of poker to be genuinely interested in hearing your bad beat stories. For my second project, I'm asking you to send me your stories for a possible book devoted exclusively to bad beat stories. Include as many details as you can.

As a third project, I'm working on a book devoted to reading poker hands, particularly hold'em hands. If you've been involved in or seen a poker hand that you think would be unusually interesting or instructive, let me know about it. Truth is stranger than fiction. Hands that were actually played in real games are usually more interesting than made-up sample hands.

It would be a pleasure to hear from you. My personal e-mail address is kennolga@earthlink.net. Thank you, in advance.

34

GLOSSARY

All-In - The act of putting all the remaining chips you have in the pot, usually before the hand is over. A player who is all-in can only win that part of the pot that he was able to match, if he has the best hand at the end.

Backdoor - Making a hand that you originally weren't drawing to, (e.g. you hold A♣ J♣, the flop is Q♥ 7♣ 3♣, the turn is the K♦, and the river is the 10♥, giving you the straight, even though you were originally hoping for the club flush after the flop.

Backraise - A reraise from a player who originally just called.

Bad Beat - To lose with a great hand—usually aces full or better—to a player who made a longshot draw.

Bankroll - The money that you have set aside to put into a poker game. This money is actually physically (or at least mentally) segregated from other money used for non-poker expenses.

Bicycle - A 5-high straight: 5432A

Big Blind - The bigger of two blinds in a game; a mandatory bet posted by the player two places to the dealer's left.

Blank - A card that is obviously of no help to a poker hand. Also called a **Brick**.

Bluff - To bet with a hand you're sure will lose if called.

Board - The cards that are turned face up in a hold'em game and belong to everybody; also called **Community Cards.**

Brick - See **Blank.**

Burn or Burn Card - After the deal and before each betting round, the top card, which is mucked by the dealer. This is done to protect everyone in the event the top card is marked or somehow known to one player while the action is in progress and everyone is waiting for that card.

Button - In casino games, a round, plastic disc with the word "Dealer" printed on each side. It moves clockwise with each new hand to indicate who holds the dealer's position.

Cards Speak - The concept that your poker hand is determined by what your cards actually are, and not by any remarks that a player may make about his hand. All casino poker games are played "cards speak," and if you turn your hand face up at the end of the hand, the dealer will read the hand for you.

Case Card - The last card of a particular rank that has not been seen during a hand and is believed to be still in the deck.

Chopping - When everyone but the two blinds folds, an agreement they make to take back their money and end the hand before the flop, thus avoiding the rake.

Cold Call - To call two or more bets at once as opposed to calling one bet and then calling another on the same round.

Community Cards - See **Board.**

GLOSSARY

Completed Hand - A poker hand that requires all five cards to make the hand. That would be a straight, a flush, a full house, four of a kind, and a straight flush.

Dominated Hand - A hand that nearly always loses when competing against another particular hand. Whenever two hold'em hands contain a common card, the hand with the higher other card dominates the other. For example, AK dominates hands like A2 and K5.

Double Belly Buster - A straight draw that has eight outs, yet is not an open-end straight draw. For example, you have 86, and the board is 10743 with one card to come. A 5 or a 9 will complete your straight.

Drawing Dead - Trying to make a particular poker hand that, even if you make it, is already beaten or cannot possibly win.

End - The fifth, and last, community card in hold'em. Also called the **River.**

Early Position - To be in the first third of the players in a hold'em game to have to act on their hands.

Flop - The first three community cards placed face up by the dealer.

Flop a Set - To have a pair in the pocket and get one more of that rank on the flop to make three of a kind, or trips.

Flush - A hand with five cards of the same suit that do not qualify as a straight flush or a royal flush.

Flush Card - A card of the suit that you need to make your flush or to pick up a flush draw.

Flush Draw - To have four cards to a flush with one or more cards to come.

Four of a Kind - A hand with four cards of matching rank, plus an extra card.

Free Card - A card received on a betting round where there turned out to be no betting on that round because everyone checked.

Freeroll - Whenever you have the nuts with more cards to come and you also have a draw to a better hand.

Full - Used to describe full houses. Whatever your three of a kind is what you are full of. 88855 is "8s full of 5s."

Full House - A hand with three cards of matching rank, plus two cards of a different matching rank.

Gutshot - An inside straight draw (e.g. you hold AK, and the flop is J107).

Implied Odds - Money that is not yet in the pot but you believe will be in the pot after you make your hand. It is an educated guess of what your pot odds will be when the hand is over.

In the Dark, Raising - Raising before you get your cards, as the blinds have to do.

Kicker - The highest card in your hand that does not help make a straight, flush, full house, or pair.

Kill - A game where the betting limits are increased (usually doubled) for the next hand only.

Late Position - To be one of the last third of the players in the game to have to act on your hand.

GLOSSARY

Limp In - To call another player's bet.

Little Blind - The smaller of the two blinds in hold'em, posted by the first player to the dealer's left before the cards are dealt.

Middle Position - To be in the middle third of the players to have to act on your hand; to have approximately an equal number of players before and after you in the play of the hand.

Muck - To fold and throw your hand in the discard pile; the discard pile itself.

Nuts - The best possible hand that can be made after the flop, the turn, and especially after the river.

On the Button - To be in the dealer's position and therefore last to act throughout each betting round of that game.

Outs - The number of cards that will help your hand. For example, if you have two hearts and get two more on the flop, there are then nine hearts (or nine outs) that will make your flush.

Overcall - A call made after there has already been a bet and a call.

Overs, Playing the - An agreement among any players in the game who want to play higher limit when there are only those players left in the hand.

Overcard - A card on the board that is higher than either of your hole cards.

Pocket - The first two cards that you're dealt that constitute your private hand.

Pot Odds - The ratio of the amount of money in the pot compared to the amount of money that is costs to call a bet. For example, if the pot contains $42 and it costs you only $3 to call, you're getting pot odds of 14-1. If it's $6 to call, you're getting pot odds of 7-1.

River - See **End**.

Rock - A poker player who has a reputation for playing only premium starting hands and whose playing style is dull, boring, and very low risk.

Royal Flush - A hand with five cards of consecutive rank, from ace to 10, all the same suit.

Rush - The experience of having won many pots close together in a short period of time.

Set - The exact situation of having a pair in the pocket and one of those cards on the board. Holding 99 with a board of 39Q is a set of 9s, but holding 39 with a board of 99Q is three 9s, but not a set.

Slowplay - To play your hand in a much weaker manner than its strength would usually call for in order to disguise that strength for a future betting round.

Spread Limit - A betting structure that allows you to bet any amount between the preset lowest and highest amounts. The most common spread limit used for hold'em is $1-$5.

Straight Draw - To have four cards to a straight with one or more cards to come.

Straddle - Occurs when the first player after the big blind raises in dark; that is, before he receives his first two cards.

GLOSSARY

Straight - A hand with five ranks in sequence.

Straight Flush - A hand with five cards of consecutive rank other than ace through 10, all the same suit.

Structured Limit - A betting structure that forces you to bet only the amount specified as the small bet and the big bet. It's usually a 1:2 ratio.

Tell - A clue from an opponent that helps you figure out what his poker hand is. That clue (or clues) can be made voluntarily or involuntarily, knowingly or unknowingly, and verbally or physically.

Three of a kind - A hand with three cards of a matching rank and two other cards whose ranks don't match.

Turn - The fourth community card in hold'em.

Two Pair - A hand with two cards of matching ranks and two other cards of a different matching rank.

Under the Gun - In first position.

Wheel - See **Bicycle**.

Zero Board - A board with which the highest possible hand is three of a kind.

GREAT CARDOZA POKER BOOKS
ADD THESE TO YOUR LIBRARY - ORDER NOW!

THE POKER TOURNAMENT FORMULA *by Arnold Snyder.* Start making money now in fast no-limit hold'em tournaments with these radical and never-before-published concepts and secrets for beating tournaments. You'll learn why cards don't matter as much as the dynamics of a tournament—your position, the size of your chip stack, who your opponents are, and above all, the structure. Poker tournaments offer one of the richest opportunities to come along in decades. Every so often, a book comes along that changes the way players attack a game and provides them with a big advantage over opponents. Gambling legend Arnold Snyder has written such a book. 368 pages, $19.95.

POKER TOURNAMENT FORMULA 2: Advanced Strategies for Big Money Tournaments *by Arnold Snyder.* Probably the greatest tournament poker book ever written, and the most controversial in the last decade, Snyder's revolutionary work debunks commonly (and falsely) held beliefs. Snyder reveals the power of chip utility—the real secret behind winning tournaments—and covers utility ranks, tournament structures, small- and long-ball strategies, patience factors, the impact of structures, crushing the Harringbots and other player types, tournament phases, and much more. Includes big sections on Tools, Strategies, and Tournament Phases. A must buy! 496 pages, $24.95.

DANIEL NEGREANU'S POWER HOLD'EM STRATEGY *by Daniel Negreanu.* This power-packed book on beating no-limit hold'em is one of the three most influential poker books ever written. Negreanu headlines a collection of young great players—Todd Brunson, David Williams. Eric Lindgren, Evelyn Ng and Paul Wasicka—who share their insider professional moves and winning secrets. You'll learn about short-handed and heads-up play, high-limit cash games, a powerful beginner's strategy to neutralize pro players, and how to mix up your play and win big pots. The centerpiece is Negreanu's powerful and revolutionary small ball strategy. You'll learn how to play hold'em with cards you never would have played before—and with fantastic results. 500 pages, $34.95.

POKER WIZARDS *by Warwick Dunnett.* In the tradition of Super System, an exclusive collection of champions and superstars have been brought together to share their strategies, insights, and tactics for winning big money at poker, specifically no-limit hold'em tournaments. This is priceless advice from players who individually have each made millions of dollars in tournaments, and collectively, have won more than 20 WSOP bracelets, two WSOP main events, 100 major tournaments and $50 million in tournament winnings! Featuring Daniel Negreanu, Dan Harrington, Marcel Luske, Kathy Liebert, Mike Sexton, Mel Judah, Marc Salem, T.J Cloutier and Chris "Jesus" Ferguson. This must-read book is a goldmine for serious players, aspiring pros, and future champions! 352 pgs, $19.95.

CARO'S BOOK OF POKER TELLS *by Mike Caro.* One of the ten greatest books written on poker, this must-have book should be in every player's library. If you're serious about winning, you'll realize that most of the profit comes from being able to read your opponents. Caro reveals the the secrets of interpreting *tells*—physical reactions that reveal information about a player's cards—such as shrugs, sighs, shaky hands, eye contact, and many more. Learn when opponents are bluffing, when they aren't and why—based solely on their mannerisms. Over 170 photos of players in action and play-by-play examples show the actual tells. These powerful ideas will give you the decisive edge. 320 pages, $24.95.

HOW TO BEAT SIT-AND-GO POKER TOURNAMENTS by Neil Timothy. There is a lot of dead money up for grabs in the lower limit sit-and-gos and Neil Timothy shows you how to go and get it. The author, a professional player, shows you how to reach the last six places of lower limit sit-and-go tournaments four out of five times and then how to get in the money 25-35 percent of the time using his powerful, proven strategies. This book can turn a losing sit-and-go player into a winner, and a winner into a bigger winner. Also effective for the early and middle stages of one-table satellites.176 pages, $14.95.

POWERFUL WINNING POKER SIMULATIONS
A MUST FOR SERIOUS PLAYERS WITH A COMPUTER!
IBM compatible CD ROM Win 95, 98, 2000, NT, ME, XP

These incredible full color poker simulations are the best method to improve your game. Computer opponents play like real players. All games let you set the limits and rake and have fully programmable players, plus stat tracking, and Hand Analyzer for starting hands. MIke Caro, the world's foremost poker theoretician says, "Amazing... a steal for under $500... get it, it's great." Includes free phone support. "Smart Advisor" gives expert advice for every play!

1. TURBO TEXAS HOLD'EM FOR WINDOWS - $59.95. Choose which players, and how many (2-10) you want to play, create loose/tight games, and control check-raising, bluffing, position, sensitivity to pot odds, and more! Also, instant replay, pop-up odds, Professional Advisor keeps track of play statistics. Free bonus: Hold'em Hand Analyzer analyzes all 169 pocket hands in detail and their win rates under any conditions you set. Caro says this "hold'em software is the most powerful ever created." Great product!

2. TURBO SEVEN-CARD STUD FOR WINDOWS - $59.95. Create any conditions of play; choose number of players (2-8), bet amounts, fixed or spread limit, bring-in method, tight/loose conditions, position, reaction to board, number of dead cards, and stack deck to create special conditions. Features instant replay. Terrific stat reporting includes analysis of starting cards, 3-D bar charts, and graphs. Play interactively and run high speed simulation to test strategies. Hand Analyzer analyzes starting hands in detail. Wow!

3. TURBO OMAHA HIGH-LOW SPLIT FOR WINDOWS - $59.95. Specify any playing conditions; betting limits, number of raises, blind structures, button position, aggressiveness/ passiveness of opponents, number of players (2-10), types of hands dealt, blinds, position, board reaction, and specify flop, turn, and river cards! Choose opponents and use provided point count or create your own. Statistical reporting, instant replay, pop-up odds high speed simulation to test strategies, amazing Hand Analyzer, and much more!

4. TURBO OMAHA HIGH FOR WINDOWS - $59.95. Same features as above, but tailored for Omaha High only. Caro says program is "an electrifying research tool...it can clearly be worth thousands of dollars to any serious player. A must for Omaha High players.

5. TURBO 7 STUD 8 OR BETTER - $59.95. Brand new with all the features you expect from the Wilson Turbo products: the latest artificial intelligence, instant advice and exact odds, play versus 2-7 opponents, enhanced data charts that can be exported or printed, the ability to fold out of turn and immediately go to the next hand, ability to peek at opponents hand, optional warning mode that warns you if a play disagrees with the advisor, and automatic mode that runs up to 50 tests unattended. Tough computer players vary their styles for a great game.

---

6. TOURNAMENT TEXAS HOLD'EM - $39.95

Set-up for tournament practice and play, this realistic simulation pits you against celebrity look-alikes. Tons of options let you control tournament size with 10 to 300 entrants, select limits, ante, rake, blind structures, freezeouts, number of rebuys and competition level of opponents. Pop-up status report shows how you're doing vs. the competition. Save tournaments in progress to play again later. Additional feature allows quick folds on finished hands.